GOD in MY LIFE

BARBARA SPEICHER

WESTBOW PRESS
A DIVISION OF THOMAS NELSON
& ZONDERVAN

Copyright © 2015 Barbara Speicher.

All rights reserved. No part of this book may be used or reproduced by any means, graphic, electronic, or mechanical, including photocopying, recording, taping or by any information storage retrieval system without the written permission of the publisher except in the case of brief quotations embodied in critical articles and reviews.

While the events are factual, some names and specific
details have been changed to protect identities.

Scripture taken from The Living Bible copyright © 1971 by Tyndale House Foundation. Used by permission of Tyndale House Publishers Inc., Carol Stream, Illinois 60188. All rights reserved. The Living Bible, TLB, and the The Living Bible logo are registered trademarks of Tyndale House Publishers.

Scripture quotations taken from the New American Standard Bible®, Copyright © 1960, 1962, 1963, 1968, 1971, 1972, 1973, 1975, 1977, 1995 by The Lockman Foundation. Used by permission. (www.Lockman.org)

WestBow Press books may be ordered through booksellers or by contacting:

WestBow Press
A Division of Thomas Nelson & Zondervan
1663 Liberty Drive
Bloomington, IN 47403
www.westbowpress.com
1 (866) 928-1240

Because of the dynamic nature of the Internet, any web addresses or links contained in this book may have changed since publication and may no longer be valid. The views expressed in this work are solely those of the author and do not necessarily reflect the views of the publisher, and the publisher hereby disclaims any responsibility for them.

Any people depicted in stock imagery provided by Thinkstock are models,
and such images are being used for illustrative purposes only.
Certain stock imagery © Thinkstock.

ISBN: 978-1-4908-7557-6 (sc)
ISBN: 978-1-4908-7559-0 (hc)
ISBN: 978-1-4908-7558-3 (e)

Library of Congress Control Number: 2015905310

Print information available on the last page.

WestBow Press rev. date: 05/05/2015

This book is dedicated to my loving husband, George,
such a caring, generous person, and devoted father.
I am so thankful for you.

When you are in love with who God is,
you will always be watching for Him.

Anonymous

CONTENTS

Preface vii
Acknowledgments ix
Introduction xi

1. The Voice of God 1
2. Why a Little Red Balloon Made a Big Difference 4
3. God Becomes Real to Me 9
4. Letter to Donna's Mother 12
5. What's Christian Music? 14
6. A Memorable Overnighter 17
7. Precious Comments 19
8. God's Truth Blessed Our Marriage 21
9. Why Can't I Hear God? 23
10. Come, and Sit Down 27
11. A Moving Moms in Touch Meeting 29
12. What Will Happen When I Die? 31
13. No Coincidence, a God-Incidence 33
14. What God Says About the Poor 36
15. God's Cleansing Power 40
16. A Prayer for My Children 42
17. Am I a Christian? 44
18. I'm Right Here 46
19. Wait and He Will Help You 49
20. Open Hearts Enter 52
21. In an Instant 54
22. John Has Hodgkin's Disease 56

23. Letter to Cecil on My Fiftieth	58
24. How Can I Help?	60
25. In His Head, Not His Heart	63
26. A Daily Walk	66
27. The Light of Day	69
28. Not Fitting In	72
29. Things are Different Now, or Are They?	75
30. My Spiritual Sacrifices	79
31. What Does Easter Mean?	82
32. We Don't Need a U-Haul	86
33. Love That Knows No Bounds	89
34. A Christmas to Remember	95
35. God's Wisdom Can Make a Change	98
36. A Mother's Prayer	101
37. Who Needs to Change?	105
38. A God of Love	108
39. Do Not Be Afraid	113
40. Deep Roots of Faith	118
41. Kevin's Search for God	123
42. Truth Marches On Regardless of Doubt	127
43. One Pathway of Truth	131
44. The Salvation Experience	134
45. A Heart for God	138
46. A Memorable Musical Moment	141
47. Let the Children Come to Me	144
48. I Understand	149
49. Our Prayers Live On	153
50. A Peaceful Passing	157
51. A Loud Voice	160
52. God Is Faithful	164
Bible Translations	172
Endnotes	173
About the Author	177

PREFACE

After months of deliberation, I finally decided to go forward with publishing my writings. I had already spoken to a representative of a book publishing company, so I made the momentous phone call to her on that Friday. How disappointing to learn that she was on vacation! I would have to wait until Monday to connect with her. Over the weekend, I couldn't believe that I started having second thoughts about this particular publishing company. Was God leading me in a different direction? On Monday I called the representative to cancel proceeding any further with them.

After taking a couple days to investigate other book publishing companies, I felt at peace, having settled on WestBow Press. I sat at my computer on that next Wednesday to make my initial call. Right at that exact moment, the phone rang. It was a call from the representative at the first publishing company. She said she had been thinking about our conversation and wanted to give me the name and phone number of a person she knew at another publishing company that she felt would be a "good fit" for me. That publishing company was (you guessed it!) WestBow Press. We both thought the timing was quite incredible. What were the odds that this would happen at that exact moment? Was God confirming my decision? I believe He was. How nice it was to be connected directly to this new person at WestBow Press. I didn't even have to make a call.

Coincidence? How many times had I experienced similar situations in my life of perfect timing, insights, and answers, the likelihood infinitesimal from a human point of view? They all confirm for me that God is actively involved if we have eyes to see and hearts that believe. In reading *God in My Life*, may you come to that same conclusion for yourself.

Acknowledgments

First and foremost, I must acknowledge God, who loves me in spite of myself and saved me by His grace. His precious Word, the Bible, has been my best teacher and source of encouragement for many years. I'm thankful for Christian writers, preachers, and friends who have shared their wisdom, helping me grow in my faith. Lastly, my gratitude overflows as I thank my husband, who has always been so supportive of my endeavors, including this one. Thank you, my love.

Introduction

I think my children know how important God is in my life. I'm constantly filled with the desire to get close to Him and know Him better. When the incessant sound of the TV permeates our family room or the beats of the latest songs are playing loudly, I steal away into my private hideaway, the office upstairs, where I can be away from the "maddening crowd." It's there that I can commune with God as I read His Word and quietly contemplate and pray.

Tacked up all over my desk and the shelves above it are meaningful quotes or sayings that serve as constant reminders of what God's will is for me, so that when my own desires direct me otherwise, I can refocus. Most of the books lining the bookshelves are religious in nature. To help engrain God's Word in my heart and mind, I have gotten into the habit of collecting my personal thoughts and writing them down. Sometimes they come in verse form; other times they are personal reflections in prose. Sometimes they are an attempt to internalize God's Word for better understanding. I don't ever want to forget about God's providence and faithfulness in my life.

Loving God, praising Him, and serving Him are my main interests in life. Naturally, when problems arise in the lives of my children, I will often suggest that they talk to God or pray about them.

One time when I made a suggestion to my son (then fifteen) to pray about a particular problem, he blurted out skeptically, "Why? I haven't seen anything that God has done for me!"

It struck me that my son was challenging me, saying, "Prove to me that God exists!" He would not be able to see and touch the nail holes in the hands and feet of Jesus, but it caused me to consider something. Could I somehow convey the reality of a living God via my personal encounters with Him?

Over the years in my own life, there had been so many times that I had felt God's Holy Spirit speaking to me through Scripture, prayer, circumstances, or other Christians. Because of their perfect timing and frequency, I could no longer call these "coincidences." Out of an intimate relationship with God, I had come to recognize His voice. I knew in my heart, with certainty, that these were "God-incidences." If I organized and compiled these personal experiences and life lessons, would my children be able to see that God is always at work around us? I knew these seemingly *ordinary* occurrences were truly *extraordinary* if one had the eyes to see.

Was it a coincidence that the same day I wrote this was the very day I just *happened* to read Deuteronomy 4:9 in my Bible that said, *"But watch out! Be careful never to forget what you have seen God doing for you. May his miracles have a deep and permanent effect upon your lives! Tell your children and your grandchildren about the glorious miracles he did."*[1] I knew that God was, once again, reaffirming His truth to me through His Word—personally, poignantly, and perfectly timed.

Originally, the reason I started keeping a record of God working in my life was for my own benefit; I never wanted to forget! I was like David in the Bible, who said, *"I shall remember the deeds of the Lord."*[2] But now it is my greatest desire to give testimony of God's faithfulness and glorious miracles through my daily experiences with Him, not only to my family, but to everyone. My hope is that all will come to know the beauty of life built on a solid foundation of knowing there is a God who loves them so much He sent His Son, Jesus, to earth to tell them, and then He died in our place so we would not be separated from God for all eternity.

All my writings are dedicated to that end—to share what God has taught me and done for me, and the lessons I have learned, as well as to demonstrate His great love, His power, and His wondrous works. I do want to be a faithful steward and follow God's leading to not forget and to *"write down for the coming generation what the Lord has done, so that people not yet born will praise him."*[3]

Heavenly Father, my earnest prayer is that all people living now, and in future generations, will come to love and glorify You and Your Son, Jesus Christ.

1

THE VOICE OF GOD

Growing up in a Christian home, I *thought* I was fairly religious. I attended church regularly and was involved in church youth activities and the choir. As I grew older, I participated in Bible studies periodically. However, it began to bother me more and more that I did not feel close to God. God seemed distant and far away. I had always professed belief in Christ, and yet I didn't feel connected to Him in a personal way. I longed for that relationship, that certainty in my life, but I constantly wrestled with the whys of religion. I wanted to be able to put everything in a neat little box, tied up with rational understanding. The more I wanted to believe, the more unanswerable questions kept popping up, throwing obstacles in my path.

One such occasion of quandary occurred when I was thirty-two and participating in a women's Bible study. All the women in my group seemed so sure of their relationship with God, but I just became more confused as each week progressed. I couldn't embrace the Bible in its entirety without reservation like everyone else. It just didn't make sense to me, and I became increasingly frustrated.

That particular week, as we studied the book of Joshua, I once again felt like an outsider. In our study, we learned that Rahab, who was a prostitute, and the people of the entire region had heard about the power of the God of Israel, and they were all afraid of Him. Rahab helped the two Israelite spies hide from the king of Jericho and his soldiers, saying, *"No wonder we are afraid of you! Your God is the supreme God of heaven, not just an ordinary god."*[1]

It seemed to me that Rahab was being swayed to Jehovah not because of her great *love* for Him, but because she *feared* His wrath and punishment. In my thinking, she was obedient to God only because she *feared* the alternative, and this just didn't seem right to me. Questions started forming in my mind: *Why would God want people to believe in Him on the basis of fear or punishment? Why would He use such a negative tactic to gain their devotion? How meaningful would a relationship based on fear be?*

This rather harsh visualization of God tormented me as I headed to my car after that day's discussion. I remember feeling both angry and confused, thinking that this Bible study was not meant for me. As I got into the car, I automatically reached for the radio dial and turned to a station I listen to frequently. Suddenly a voice that was bigger than life enveloped the car. It was so loud and overwhelming that I couldn't move. I felt as if I could hardly breathe. The voice was that of Chuck Smith, a familiar local pastor, but it had volume and power that were not of this world. The topic being discussed right then and there was why God uses fear, along with love, to gain our allegiance. I was transfixed. Was God trying to talk to me? I immediately grabbed a piece of paper and wrote down as much as I could.

I listened intently. The message conveyed was that some people don't respond to God unless they are shaken up in their complacency and static existence. God would probably always choose to use loving means, but that doesn't always work. The pastor compared God to a parent whose child constantly chooses to disobey unless threatened with severe measures or given proper punishment. Continuing, he said that God knows what is best for us, but we can only see with partial vision and scope. Sometimes what seems cruel and unjust (as a child's limited understanding of his parent's punishment toward him) is actually for our own good in the long run. God is infinitely wise, all-knowing, and all-loving. The pastor ended with words from Isaiah: *"No one can fathom the depth of His understanding."*[2]

That was true. We view life in a very restricted capacity. Hadn't I been looking at all these Bible stories through human eyes? Just like the Pharisees, I was not seeing the deity of God, but only His humanity. I had just experienced His awesome power and incredible love, even with all my frailties and shortcomings. I was getting a personal glimpse of His magnitude because I was persistent in seeking Him, even in all my confusion. As the Bible promises, *"You will find me when you seek me if you look for me in earnest."*[3]

As I look back on this incident now, it seems unreal. And yet, isn't that the point? God doesn't deal on the level of the natural. He is beyond that. He is bigger than any of us can imagine. All of this *did* happen. I have a vivid memory of it, especially because I realize with assuredness that God cares about me. I can still recall the overwhelming emotions I felt driving home that day: a mixture of reverence and humbleness along with great amazement. There was no doubt in my mind that God had spoken to me personally.

Lord, thank you for this awesome, incredible moment.

2

WHY A LITTLE RED BALLOON MADE A BIG DIFFERENCE

It was May 1985, and I was five months pregnant with my third child. As each day progressed and my dimensions increased noticeably, I grew more and more excited. Because I was thirty-five years old, my doctor had recommended that I have an amniocentesis, but liking surprises, I had asked not to be informed about the results of the sex. Little did I know that coming in that month of May was an unwanted surprise that would be shocking and life-changing for my entire family!

One afternoon, unexpectedly, we received a frantic call from my mother, who informed us that my father had just experienced a massive heart attack at Lake Havasu, Arizona. My parents own a recreational mobile home there, a place where our all of us "kids" and the grandchildren had spent many happy times together. This news stunned us all, as my dad was in perfect health at sixty-five (so we thought) and had just received a clean bill of health from his doctor at his very recent physical. In fact, he had just spent the day before waterskiing and painting the interior of their mobile home. There had never been any warning signs.

Unsettled, we waited for further phone calls, not knowing whether we should rush out to Lake Havasu or just sit and wait. We felt very helpless and empty. My mom called again, this time to tell us that Dad was being airlifted to a hospital near their home. Heartbroken, she mentioned that 60 percent of his heart had been damaged and it was difficult to determine at this point whether he would make it or not. The only thing we could do was wait and pray.

I had grown up with a churchgoing family, and I knew how to pray, but I couldn't honestly say at the age of thirty-five that I knew God personally, felt His closeness, or knew for certain that He was really there listening to me. (How quickly I had forgotten the "Voice of God" incident!) Much of my communication had more of an "If you're there, God …" approach. I prayed my heart out, but the essence still seemed hollow. I was so overwhelmed with worry and grief that I had a difficult time finding the words I felt were adequate to express my feelings to God.

Once my father had been transferred nearby, my family was allowed to see him for a very short visit. My husband; my oldest daughter, Kim; and I talked to him briefly. We could not get our son Kevin to see his grandfather. Kevin was extremely upset, for Grandpa had been his fishing buddy. His only request for his fifth birthday was to go fishing with his grandfather. Grandma and Grandpa had bought Kevin a well-equipped tackle box and matching hats for the two of them. We had invested in a nice fishing pole. The birthday plan was for just the two of them to spend the day together, fishing to their hearts' content, something they both loved to do.

These plans would have to be postponed. I think it was just too much for Kevin to see his energetic and robust grandfather lying helplessly in a hospital bed with tubes running every which way. As much as we prodded, we could never get Kevin to see his grandpa. He just kept saying he wanted to remember Grandpa the way he was. The rest of us all had great hope for his recovery, but the intuition of a young child perceived a different vision of the future.

After several more days, my father was taken by ambulance to a more specialized hospital with the most up-to-date medical technology, where he would receive the best attention available. A surgery was needed to insert a balloon next to his heart to help it beat properly because it had been damaged so extensively and was having difficulty performing on its own. At one point his heart completely stopped, and doctors and nurses rushed to his bedside to get it pumping again. We just took one day at a time, not being sure of what the next day held.

Almost two weeks had passed since the initial heart attack. We knew that even if Dad survived, his life would be completely different. With 60 percent of his heart damaged, he would be forced to be more sedentary, a word not synonymous with my dad. Would this man—who could have played professional baseball had he not chosen a career in teaching, who had been a high school football coach and swimming instructor, and who was an avid outdoorsman—be able to cope with such a sudden change? We all knew he'd have no choice, but would he really be happy?

My mother and I were making frequent trips to see him. He was an hour's drive away, and several times, my mother stayed overnight at the hospital to be near my dad. Wednesday night, exactly two weeks after the heart attack, we were debating about spending the night. My father had been having some difficulty, but he was resting, so the nurses encouraged us to go home and get some sleep. I saw him for just a brief moment before we left. At first I didn't think he was aware I was in the room, but then he opened his eyes sleepily and whispered, "My wonderful daughter, I'm so proud of you. You know I will always love you." My eyes filled with tears, for I knew he was the best father any girl could have, and I loved him very much. He just had to live! To think otherwise was unbearable.

Death was not at all in my thinking as I left the hospital with my mother that evening. We had just gotten in the door when the hospital called and told us to come back immediately. Things had taken a turn for the worse. My mother and I sped back to the hospital, and when we arrived, we heard the doctor's sad pronouncement we were dreading: "Alvin Curtis Searfoss passed away at ten thirty this evening." This was only one and one-half hours away from Kevin's birthday, the birthday the two of them had hoped to spend together fishing. I thought about how sad not only Kevin would be, but also our whole family and everyone else who knew and loved this wonderful man, now gone from our lives.

We were all in shock and disbelief during the following days. We made it through the memorial service, but it would take a while for the reality of this loss to sink in. We carried that dull pain of emptiness and sorrow in our hearts. I would pray to God, "I hope You are taking good care of my father," not really feeling very sure in my heart about anything anymore.

Three months later, after my father's death, our third child, Katie, was born. It was a happy occasion after such grief we had all experienced. This new life was helping to fill the void of loss. Kevin began kindergarten that year. Kim was in second grade. To welcome the new school year, Nelson Elementary School, where they attended, held a balloon launch one afternoon. Kim and Kevin were very excited as their two colorful balloons joined the seven hundred others winding their way up into the clear blue sky over the neighborhood houses. Each day, the school would report where one had been discovered and pinpoint it on a map. Kim's came back a few days later with a nice note attached that read as follows:

> Dear Kim,
> Hi, my name is Sharon. I live in the valley of Perris, California. We are located about two miles west of Perris Lake. We live in a country-like area upon a hill. I was working in our fruit tree field when I found your burst balloon and card. It gave our family such joy to know you had launched your balloon at school, and it had traveled all the way to our home in Perris Valley. Kim, thank you for touching our hearts with your yellow balloon.
> Thanks again,
Sharon

This happy little message coming from a place about fifty miles away from our home lifted all of our spirits that day. However, nothing could match the emotion that I felt when Kevin's card was returned to school a few days later. His little red balloon had traveled all the way to (Are you ready?) Lake Havasu, Arizona! In fact, Kevin's balloon went the farthest of all the balloons of the children in the entire school, a distance of about three hundred miles! Out of seven hundred balloons, Kevin's ended up in Lake Havasu, where our family spent many happy times together and where his grandfather had his heart attack!

I knew in my heart that this was no coincidence. For me it was a sign from God and from my father, each saying together, "I love you, and I will always be with you." I felt God's overwhelming presence at that moment, and I just kept saying, "Thank you, Lord, thank you. You have answered my prayers. My father is safe in Your arms, and you are there for him, for me, and for everyone if we just trust You and believe."

Lord, You know that my father's death brought me much sadness and grief, but I just want to praise You because it also brought me closer to You. You didn't move a mountain, but you moved a little red balloon, and that has made all the difference!

November 1985

3
GOD BECOMES REAL TO ME

For some reason, even after experiencing "God-incidences" in my life, which should have been impactful enough to be life-changing, I still felt disconnected. I began to bring up more and more questions: Was God really personally involved in our lives (and this was not long after the balloon incident)? Did He really care? Was Jesus really God incarnate? I was frustrated, once again, because I didn't have that peace of certainty.

In my mind, I reasoned that either Jesus was who He said He was in the Bible (the Son of God), or He was a fake, an imposter, and the Bible itself was basically just a fairytale. There were really no other choices! To my surprise, the next time we attended church, the minister spoke on that very subject: "Jesus, Son of God or Mad-Man." The minister spoke of the fact that almost all the disciples of Jesus died as martyrs, a pretty strong commitment from a group of followers backing a lunatic. Also, he pointed out the many prophesies (over three hundred) that speak of the genuineness of Jesus, that have been fulfilled through Him, and that continue to validate His legitimacy. Was God speaking to me again?

Not much later, we were attending church one Sunday when the minister said something that really made an impact on me. He suggested that in order to get close to God, we should stand in front of a mirror, looking at ourselves, and with our hands cupped together in front of us, make this simple plea: "God, take all that I'm not and put it into all that You are." I left the service knowing that I needed to make that request.

Later that evening, I did just what the minister suggested. I walked over to a mirror and stood in front of it. With my hands cupped together in front of me, I took a good look at myself. Standing there staring at myself, I started saying that phrase over and over: "God, take all that I'm not, and put it into all that You are." The more I said it, the more I began to see how small I was, how insignificant, how needy, and how much I desperately needed to be saved from myself. Tears of brokenness started falling down my face, and pretty soon I was sobbing, crying, "I am nothing, Lord, nothing, and you are everything! Forgive me, Jesus. I need You so much." It was as if God were staring back at me from the mirror and showing me my failings, my flaws, my insufficiency and my need to be saved. I felt so small and totally humbled, realizing who I was compared to God. I just gave my whole life over to God. Lightning didn't strike at that moment, but I do remember afterward having a sense of peace and expectancy. I would patiently wait for an answer.

Answers did start coming when, several nights later, I was startled out of my sleep by a vision of myself dying. It was so real. Within myself I heard a voice saying, "God, it's not time. I have so much yet to do!" And I knew that I didn't just mean busy, mundane activities and pursuits. I meant my special work for God here on earth. At that point I really felt that my life was going to be different. I began to look for ways to make my life meaningful, to be used by God for His purposes, and to help other people. This would be the beginning of my journey with God. I was willing and ready.

I thank God that He was so faithful over the years of my searching and seeking. Even at those times when I knew, without a doubt, that He was demonstrating His living presence to me, I continued to be hardheaded and hard-hearted. He didn't give up on me even though I walked away from Him many times.

Thank you, Lord, that in Your mercy and compassion You saw through that prideful facade to my heart that yearned to know You personally and be close to You. You are an awesome, loving God. I praise You that You faithfully kept Your promise to me:

GOD BECOMES REAL TO ME

... you will seek the Lord your God, and you will find Him if you search for Him with all your heart and all your soul.
(Deuteronomy 4:29 NASB)

February 1986

4

LETTER TO DONNA'S MOTHER

The following is a letter I wrote to my friend's mother when she was in the hospital, dying of cancer. I felt a real urgency to get the letter to my friend right after writing it, so I drove it over to her house that very day.

Jan. 6, 1987

Dear Mrs. DeCubelis,

    I wanted to share some thoughts with you and am asking Donna to read this to you in the hospital.

    For about a year now, not long after my father's death, I have felt that God is a very real presence in my life. Every day I try to listen to Him and keep my mind open to what He might have to say to me. Last Sunday evening, I was thinking about you and once again was confounded by the seeming injustices of disease, pain, and suffering. Right at that moment, I turned on the T.V. and flipped through the channels, but stopped suddenly when I heard this minister preaching on the subject of suffering.

    I felt a need to tell you some of the things he said. He stated that we will probably never completely understand why there is suffering until one day when we meet the Almighty and all will be made clear. We don't always see the end of the tunnel, but we can still praise and trust God.

Letter to Donna's Mother

The minister relayed three assurances from the Bible that we can know in regard to suffering. First, God precedes us in our suffering. He's been there ahead of us. He was betrayed and He suffered on the cross. Secondly, God joins us in our suffering. He walks with us through the storm. Last of all, God Himself will bring us through our suffering; *"nothing can ever separate us from His love. Death can't and life can't. Our fears for today, our worries about tomorrow or where we are, high above the sky, or in the deepest ocean – nothing will ever be able to separate us from the love of God demonstrated by our Lord Jesus Christ when He died for us."*[1]

I am so saddened by your illness. You brought into the world one of my dearest friends and I will always be grateful to you for that. May God lay His comforting hands upon you and bring you peace.

Love,
Barbara

Donna read this letter to her mother that evening. Her mother died later that night.

5

WHAT'S CHRISTIAN MUSIC?

It was the first week of May. My oldest daughter, Kim, and two of her friends decided to participate in the upcoming talent show at their elementary school and had picked out a song made popular by a contemporary Christian artist. I was so thrilled that they had decided to sing this upbeat song about the love of Jesus to the other students. Since the other girls came from strong Christian families, I knew their parents would be excited, too.

To my amazement, however, Kim came home from their first practice saying that one girl's mother felt that the song was "too rock 'n' roll" and decided that the girls should dance a Hawaiian number wearing little grass skirts instead. I was stunned! Here was a great opportunity for the girls to witness about their love for Jesus to the entire school, and because of one mother's opinion, they were being swayed otherwise. Kim and I talked about it that night, and since she had her heart set on singing this particular song, she decided to sing it alone.

During the next few days, I was preoccupied by this mother's insistence that this song was "too rock 'n' roll." I had often played this artist's albums, which I felt drew me closer to God, and I had always viewed the songs as a positive influence, especially for young people who love upbeat contemporary music. Was my anger justified?

The answer came to me that Saturday night at 10:30 p.m. as I was leaving in the car to head to the grocery store. I punched the button to one of the Christian radio stations I listen to, but there was complete silence. I thought, *How strange!* I switched to a different station and then back again to see if anything would come up. Once more, there was nothing. So I switched to another station just in time to hear the broadcaster announce their next topic for discussion: "What Do You Think about Christian Rock 'n' Roll?" I quickly grabbed a scrap of paper I found on the floor of my car under the seat and searched for a pen in my purse as, once again, I knew God wanted me to hear this message.

Under discussion was the fact that the main concern about Christian rock 'n' roll centered on several questions: Is it good for Christian music to conform to the secular world? Are we imitating evil? The main response from callers seemed to be that we have to listen carefully to the lyrics. Is a clear message being preached? Is it glorifying and edifying Christ? Many callers testified to the fact that they had accepted Christ at concerts given by not only Christian rock 'n' roll artists, but even heavy metal Christian groups. These young people testified that we are living in aggressive times, and they felt that many of these groups are more "on fire" for Christ. Is a person less Christian if he accepts Christ through rock 'n' roll music rather than any other way? Not just a momentary emotion, but the remaining fruit or abiding desire for Jesus Christ would attest to that truth.

Many callers felt that there must be more cohesiveness among Christians and less narrow thinking, as we can get a strong Christian message by many avenues, one not necessarily being better or more appropriate than another. We are all individuals and different, and we are allowed to be ourselves as long as we allow God to be number one in our lives. One caller even said she wished people weren't so quick to judge. It's true that God just wants us to plant a seed, and only He knows our hearts and our motives.

Later, I found several psalms in the Bible (LB) that emphasize the importance and power of unique and diverse music in praising and glorifying God:

- *Hallelujah! Yes, praise the Lord! Sing him a new song. Sing his praises, all his people ...* (149:1)
- *Praise his name with dancing, accompanied by drums and lyre.* (149:3)

- *Praise him with the trumpet and with lute and harp. Praise him with the tambourines and processional. Praise him with stringed instruments and horns. Praise him with the cymbals; yes, loud clanging cymbals. Let everything alive give praises to the Lord! You praise him! Hallelujah!* (150:3–6)
- *He has given me a new song to sing of praises to our God. Now many will hear of the glorious things he did for me, and stand in awe before the Lord, and put their trust in him.* (40:3)

The Bible says that before Christ comes again, *"the Good News about the Kingdom will be preached throughout the whole world, so that all nations will hear it."*[1] Different types of music allow the gospel to be presented where it never has been before. It's one more powerful way to make inroads and draw people to God. Rick Warren, evangelical Christian pastor and author, stated, "God loves all kinds of music because He invented it all: fast and slow, loud and soft, old and new ... If it is offered to God in spirit and truth, it is an act of worship ... there is no such thing as Christian music, there are only Christian lyrics."[2]

When I arrived home from the grocery store later that night, out of curiosity, I switched back to the first radio station that had been silent. A song was playing.

Lord, great is Your love; great is Your power. Please help us be gracious in our love of others. Help us to be more like Jesus and more tolerant of those different than we are without compromising our beliefs and principles. Help us to remember always that You are the reason for our being. We live to be Your good and faithful servants in whatever capacity You desire for our lives. It's all about You. We live for Your glory.

May 1987

6

A Memorable Overnighter

It was October 3 and the Girl Scout troop of fourth graders I led was having an overnighter at a Girl Scout beach house. Upon our arrival we discovered that our accommodations did not include beds, so the fifteen girls and three chaperones, carefully selected individual hardwood floor spots and arranged their sleeping bags. Sleeping without padding made the impact of what occurred in those early morning hours even more pronounced. A 5.5 earthquake hit at 4:00 a.m.

Being responsible for so many individuals, my first reaction was sheer panic. I shouted to get under tables; however, everyone was completely disoriented and half asleep. It was difficult to see in the dark, and some of the girls started to cry. In the midst of the confusion, my daughter Kim, sensing my fear, looked at me confidently and stated, "You know, Mom, we're in God's hands."

I immediately felt a calm come over me as I began moving about, reassuring the girls that everything would be all right. Thank goodness for little voices reminding us of simple truths.

Since then, this episode has made me more cognizant of certain Biblical facts that yes, ultimately God is in control. God set the world in motion (Genesis 1 and 2). He has fixed the laws of nature, as indicated in Jeremiah, where He says, *"I would no longer reject my people than I would change my laws of night and day, of earth and sky."*[1]

God *could* interrupt those laws if He so chose. Some examples in the Bible are when *"the sun and the moon didn't move until the Israeli army had finished the destruction of its enemies,"*[2] and another occasion when God performed a miracle and moved the shadow of the sundial backward when it had always moved forward.[3] Also, the Bible indicates in Matthew that at the time of Christ's death on the cross, in the *"afternoon, the whole earth was covered with darkness for three hours, from noon until three o'clock."*[4] It further states, *"The curtain secluding the Holiest Place in the Temple was split apart from top to bottom; and the earth shook, and rocks broke ..."*[5] Later, when Paul and Silas had been imprisoned because of their faith in Christ and were singing hymns of praise to God, *"suddenly there came a great earthquake, so that the foundations of the prison house were shaken; and immediately all the doors were opened and everyone's chains were unfastened."*[6]

We cannot understand all that God does and doesn't do. The Bible explains that His thoughts and ways are much higher than ours.[7] However, we can be like David in the Bible who said, *"I have set the Lord continually before Me; Because He is at my right hand, I will not be shaken."*[8] We can have the comforting assurance that God loves us, that He cares about us, that He has a plan and purpose for our lives, and that His greatest desire is for us to have a personal relationship with Him through His son, Jesus Christ.

Heavenly Father, there are many things we do not understand, and with our limited capacity we never will until we meet you face-to-face. Give us faith to believe in the greatness of Your power. We ask all in the name of Your Son, Jesus. Amen!

> *"For the mountains may be removed and the hills may shake, but my lovingkindness will not be removed from you and my covenant of peace will not be shaken," says the Lord who has compassion on you.*
>
> Isaiah 54:10 NASB

October 1987

7
PRECIOUS COMMENTS

How blessed I have been as a mother to see my third child, Katie, happily and openly expressing her love for Jesus. At the age of seven, she asked if she could be baptized, and all on her own, she went through the prebaptism class. After that, she gave her personal testimony in front of our rather large church congregation one Sunday morning. I was very proud of her as she bravely stood in her robe in the water with the Sunday school pastor next to her. She did not seem afraid but spoke out confidently that Jesus had come to live in her heart and she wanted everyone to know.

Over the last several years, I have written down some of her memorable comments showing her close relationship with her friend Jesus. They are precious and sweet, and they always bring a smile to my face.

- A mother helper at Katie's preschool said that Katie (age four) had gotten into a scuffle with another child at preschool—fists flying, feet kicking. The mother helper pulled Katie aside and encouraged her to apologize, at which she balked. After several futile attempts at reconciliation, the mother threw up her hands and in exasperation asked, "Well, Katie, then what should we do?" Katie calmly replied, "Well, maybe we should pray."
- Katie (age four) and I were saying prayers together one night. We took turns sharing our thoughts. In closing, I stopped after

saying "A ..." waiting for her to continue with "men." Instead her eyes focused on her alphabet chart on the wall behind us, and she continued, "b, c, d, e ..."

- Our family was out at Lake Havasu with our relatives. As usual upon arriving, Grandma put the flag out in remembrance of Grandpa, who had died when I was carrying Katie. One day, out of curiosity, Katie's oldest cousin, Elisa, asked her if she knew why the flag was there. Confidently (at age four), she answered, "It is there for God, Jesus, and Grandpa!"
- Katie (age five) and I were riding in the car while a Christian radio station was playing. A lady was recounting an experience where she had been angry with God. Katie had a hard time understanding that possibility, but in an attempt to relate, she said, "You know, God tricked me one time." I asked, "How?" She explained, "I tripped and didn't see anything, so God must have done it!"
- Katie (age five) was showering one evening, busily and carefully washing her cross necklace. Kim, her older sister, asked Katie what she was doing. Katie matter-of-factly stated, "I'm washing God." Then, as she continued the cleaning, she further explained, "Now I'm washing His hair!"
- Katie (age seven) asked to say grace one evening and was doing a very nice job. We often ask God to use our food to nourish our bodies. Katie contributed her own version of the request when she said, "Lord, help this food to nourish our bottoms! Amen."
- Katie (age seven) was saying her prayers tonight, and every sentence had the word "me" in it. "Lord, help me sing well in my play tomorrow. Help make my cold go away. Help me read better." I suggested, "Why don't we pray for someone else." Katie thought about it and added, "Lord, help my mother have a good time with *me* tomorrow."

August 1992

8
God's Truth Blessed Our Marriage

Loving God so much and putting Him first in my life has its challenges, especially when others around me do not share that same desire. That is why I often steal myself away to the private confines of our office upstairs to be with God alone, unhindered and inconspicuous. There I can read my Bible, pray, and praise God in my own way, expressing my adoration openly and uninhibited.

I remember being especially frustrated one evening with my husband's indifference to God and His Word. Just a few minutes previously, I had been so filled with love and joy after having spent time reading the Bible and in prayer, and now I was feeling out of sorts and discouraged. How could George seem so indifferent to things pertaining to God? Wasn't this more important than the other more trivial preoccupations of life? This spiritual pursuit seemed to be way down on the list of priorities in his life. God was so important to me, but the more I embraced my faith, the further George seemed to be driven away. In all honesty, it was hard to show my genuine affection toward him at those times when I felt so frustrated.

That night I went to bed feeling a giant wedge between us. I lay there sleepless. Exasperated, I got up, drawn to the sanctuary of the office walls. I tried praying but couldn't focus, so I picked up my Bible and randomly started reading Matthew 7 (LB). It stated (with my interjections added),

> *Don't criticize, and then you won't be criticized. For others will treat you as you treat them. And why worry about a speck in the eye of a brother* [or husband] *when you have a board in your own. Should you say, "Friend (Husband) let me help you," get that speck out of your eye," when you have a board in your own? Hypocrite! First get rid of the board. Then you can see to help your brother* [husband].
> (Matthew 7:1–5)

Wow, I thought to myself, *is God trying to tell me something?* All this time I had been focusing on *my* desires, *my* needs, everything George wasn't, and had not even considered that I might be part of the problem. Was I heeding God's instruction in His Word to be patient, loving, kind, and merciful? Was I following Christ's selfless example of unconditional love whether I felt like it or not? Everything was being made clear. I needed to humble myself, see the board in my own eye, and confess my sin.

I knew God was speaking to me. God always desires love, peace, and harmony; not anger, resentment, and brokenness. It was obvious to me right then and there that the root of our marriage, and probably many other relationships, was selfishness—totally looking at things from a one-way self-absorbed perspective. Only God would be able to change George's heart, and my piercing arrows of bitterness and condemnation weren't going to help. I vowed I wouldn't let Satan drive that destructive wedge of disenchantment and doubt any further between us.

I went back to bed with a whole different outlook. God's Word is good. It is truth, the essence of real love. I reached over and gave George a big hug even though he was sound asleep. Then I thanked God for George and my many blessings.

May 1993

9

WHY CAN'T I HEAR GOD?

Through my children's formative years as they were growing up, I would often tell them to stop for a few quiet moments and listen to God's voice. Sometimes they would comment that they couldn't hear God talking to them; that they didn't feel His presence or know if He was listening. I understood what they were saying, for there was a time in my past when I was uncertain if God was really there listening to my prayers.

The Bible directs us to ask this important question: *"How do we hear God if we do not belong to Him?"*[1] Belonging to God means surrendering to God and loving Him with our whole heart, without question or reservation. It means asking Him to remove anything from our lives that stands in the way of that perfect union. Belonging to Him means eliminating a lot of superficial and temporary things that fill up our lives, and refilling that empty space with Him.

The Bible explains: just as *"no one can know what anyone else is really thinking except that person alone, no one can know God's thoughts except God's own Spirit."*[2] The moment we humbly and sincerely accept His Son as our Savior, God gives us His Holy Spirit so we can understand God's thoughts and ways.[3] It's then that we will hear His voice because we become one with Him. If God's Spirit is within us with synonymous thoughts of the Father, we need to quiet our minds and listen so we can hear and think God's thoughts. The Spirit is omnipresent, our minds being one of those places always working in perfect unity and harmony with God's will.

Jesus knew this oneness in Spirit with the Father, as He speaks about it often throughout the gospel of John (NASB).

> *Truly, truly I say to you, the Son can do nothing of Himself.* (5:19)

> *I can do nothing on My own initiative ... I do not seek My own will, but the will of Him who sent Me.* (5:30)

> *My teaching is not Mine, but His who sent Me.* (7:29)

> *... I do nothing on My own initiative, but I speak these things as the Father taught Me.* (8:28b)

> *He who sent Me is with Me. He has not left Me alone, for I always do the things that are pleasing to Him.* (8:29)

> *I do not speak on my own initiative, but the Father Himself who sent Me has given me a commandment as to what to say and what to speak.* (12:48)

> *The words I say to you I do not speak on my own initiative ...* (14:10c)

> *... for all things that I have heard from my Father I have made known to you.* (15:15b)

> *... I am not alone because the Father is with Me.* (16:32b)

> *You, Father, are in Me and I in You that they also may be in us.* (17:21)

The disciples of Jesus also knew this oneness in the Spirit. Their awareness of the Holy Spirit's leading is evident throughout the book of Acts in the formation of the early church. It doesn't say God's voice was audible, but because they were constantly seeking direction from the Holy Spirit and listening, in their minds, they knew.

While they were ministering to the Lord and fasting, the Holy Spirit said, "Set apart for Me Barnabas and Saul for the work to which I have called them." (13:2)

So, being sent out by the Holy Spirit, they went down to Selecia and from there they sailed to Cyprus. (13:4)

But Saul, who was also known as Paul, filled with the Holy Spirit, fixed his gaze on him (Elymas, the magician), and said you "are full of all deceit and fraud, you son of the devil." (13:9)

And the disciples were continually filled with joy and with the Holy Spirit. (13:52)

They passed through the Phrygian and Galatian region, having been forbidden by the Holy Spirit to speak the word in Asia. (16:6)

Afterwards, Paul felt impelled by the Holy Spirit to go across to Greece before returning to Jerusalem. (19:21 LB)

And now, behold, bound in the Holy Spirit, I am on my way to Jerusalem, not knowing what will happen to me there. (20:22)

After looking up the disciples, we stayed there seven days; and they kept telling Paul through the Spirit, not to set foot in Jerusalem. (21:4)

Agabus, a prophet, came to us and took Paul's belt and bound his own feet and hands, and said, "This is what the Holy Spirit says: In this way the Jews at Jerusalem will bind the man who owns this belt and deliver him into the hands of the Gentiles." (21:11)

The Holy Spirit guides, directs, and teaches. Jesus told His disciples, "*But the Helper, the Holy Spirit, whom the Father will send in My name,*

He will teach you all things ..."[4] This verse doesn't say "a few things"; it says "*all things*"!

How do we become students of this instruction? We need quietness and stillness, which are alien words in our culture (especially for kids), to hear the exchange and gain godly wisdom and understanding. From personal experience, I knew it was in the quiet times when I was still and listening in expectation of hearing, that God gave me insights and direction. Just as God said to Moses, "... *stand by Me, that I may speak to you ...,*"[5] if we take time to allow the Spirit in us to communicate God's thoughts to us while we are focused on listening, God tells us there will be power, there will be results, and we will hear.

It's important for me to tell my children that if they want to hear God's voice, they need to draw near to Him and humbly pray,

> Lord, I ask that You take away my sins that keep me far from You. I desire less and less of myself while You become greater within me. Help me to feel Your loving presence. Take me, cleanse, me, and fill me with Your Holy Spirit. I submit my life to You. I want to know You better and clearly hear Your voice. Help me to "*be still, and know that (You are) God.*"[6] I will wait, and I will listen.

June 1995

10

COME, AND SIT DOWN

After two and half weeks of attempting to recover from a painful surgery, I decided I should be able to pick up a few groceries at a supermarket nearby. Because it was still difficult for me to be on my feet for any length of time, I asked my ten-year-old son, Kevin, to come along as my cart pusher. After journeying down only two aisles of the store, I knew I needed to sit down. I just stood there feeling miserable, hurting so badly. I couldn't take another step. I even stooped down, pretending to look at items on the lower shelves just to sit on my haunches for a while and relieve the pressure. Kevin realized my painful predicament. He took a quick look around and spied a beach chair for sale above one of the top shelves. He excitedly announced that he would get the chair down and I could sit on it in the aisle as we pretended to discuss buying it.

I hesitated at first, wondering, *What will people think? Should I just try to hobble out of the store in pain or continue a few steps at a time with frequent rests, relying on sheer fortitude and perseverance?*

That chair sure looked inviting, and I needed to rest. Exhausted and hurting, and unable to move forward, I acquiesced. With the big decision made, Kevin pulled the chair down, and there I sat in the middle of the aisle while we pretended to discuss all of its fine features. All pride, ego, and importance of outward appearance vanished as I sat resting in that chair. After having a few minutes to sit and regroup, I was able to get up and amble out of the store and back to the car.

Now, years later, I look back on that experience with an inward chuckle. However, I also see something else: a picture of God and myself, or anyone else for that matter. We're all walking through the aisles of life, looking for rest and peace of mind. We race past this and that in our busyness, and at other times trudge slowly, growing tired and frustrated. That's where I was in the grocery store—feeling as though I couldn't take another step. When my resourceful son pointed out the chair, I could have stopped and stared at it, even admired it, for I believed it would support me, but my rest didn't come until I acted upon my belief and actually walked over and plopped down in it.

Faith in God can be compared to the chair illustration. I can agree intellectually that the chair exists and will support me if I sit in. But I do not actually experience that supportive relationship until I act on my belief and put my life in that chair—or, in essence, God's hands. I have to walk past pride, ego, and worldly influences and pressures, and make a purposeful decision of the will; I must act on my belief to experience the truth personally. That faith involves reliance and dependence, not just intellectual agreement. With that rest comes freedom and peace, a new beginning. For me in the store, I knew I could start afresh, for I had overcome pride and self-reliance, and I found hope and comfort when I made the decision to sit in a chair that was just waiting there. God is always waiting, too. He invites everyone to "come and sit down."

July 1995

11

A Moving Moms in Touch Meeting

It was a Tuesday morning in April, and I was sitting in the living room of Tina's house, where our weekly Moms in Touch prayer meeting was held. Our goal was to regularly pray for about an hour, concentrating on our children and their schools. There were only three of us in attendance that day. We began our prayer time by praising God and thanking Him. As we proceeded, I could hear the voices of my friend's teenage children in conversation upstairs. I found myself becoming more and more annoyed, as I was easily getting distracted. As much as I tried to block the noise out, I was having great difficulty staying focused. I was thinking to myself, *Can't her kids see we're having a prayer meeting and be more courteous?*

Once again, the hoped-for quietude was interrupted by the jangling of the kitchen phone. Soon after that, the front door opened and in walked Tina's husband. At least he noticed what we were doing and strode up the stairs without comment. I was so disconcerted at that point, however, that I think I heard every step he took (although he really wasn't being very loud). After that, there were a few other intermittent interruptions.

Somehow, when our prayer time had concluded, I didn't feel especially connected to God; nor did I feel we had accomplished much. I was just about to make an offhand comment about the constant interruptions to try and make a point, but unexpectedly, out of my mouth came "Tina, it is so nice of you and your family to have us here every week. It must be very hard for them to have us invade your home."

I was quite dumbfounded at the softer words that came out of my mouth, for I had really felt quite the opposite. It suddenly struck me that God was tapping me on the shoulder and saying, "Do you understand now?" Just as 1 Corinthians 2:13 explains, *"We have even used the very words given to us by the Holy Spirit, not words that we as men might use."*[1]

God was giving me a firsthand example in an everyday situation of what Galatians 5:19–22 is all about. We have two forces within us that are constantly fighting for control. When we follow our own inclination, our lives will produce selfishness, anger, jealousy, complaints, criticism, resentment, bitterness, and the feeling that everyone else is wrong. But when the Holy Spirit controls our lives, it will produce *"love, joy, peace, patience, kindness, goodness, gentleness, and self-control."*[2] I privately thanked God for making it so clear to me and for giving me the power to control my own inclinations.

My friend was obviously relieved with my comment, for it suddenly occurred to me how embarrassed she must have felt about the constant interruptions. We were actually invading *their* privacy, and how *we* responded could be a witness to her entire family.

I think this incident also showed me how we can communicate with God not only in solitude but also in the chaotic moments of everyday living. He's always there, drawing us to Him, wanting us to learn to put into practice His Word by the power of His loving Holy Spirit, being a genuine Christian. Doesn't the suffix "-ian" mean "to resemble"? If we say we are Christ*ian*, we are to resemble Christ!

Lord, thank You for the constant companion of Your Holy Spirit. Oh, how we need You to be in us to show unselfish love, and to act as Your Son, Jesus Christ. We can't do it alone!

April 1996

12

WHAT WILL HAPPEN WHEN I DIE?

One July day, my sister-in-law called me because she was concerned that her four-year old son was overly preoccupied with death and dying. Having gone through this stage with our son when he was about the same age, I tried to reassure my sister-in-law that this was not unusual. A child's awareness of death at that age could create some major fears, as well as a lot of crying.

As we continued to talk, I so wanted to further reassure my confused young nephew, and also his mother, that when we have Christ in our hearts we do not need to be afraid, for He will always take care of us no matter what; but reluctantly, I held back. From experience, I didn't want to overstep my bounds when it came to discussing religion with my relatives, as I knew it could put a further wedge between us.

I was still thinking about my nephew the next morning when I was flipping through the Bible and just "happened" to stop and read from the book of Ecclesiastes. This is a book in the Bible I rarely read, so why I chose it to read it right then was beyond me. "Beyond me" was so true! After reading chapter seven in the Bible, I know once again that God does not operate in the field of coincidences. This passage was poignant and definitely pertinent.

> *For you are going to die, and it is a good thing to think about it while there is still time.* (Ecclesiastes 7:2a LB)

God in My Life

Yes, a wise man thinks much of death, while the fool thinks only of having a good time now. (Ecclesiastes 7:4 LB)

God's truth is alive and personal, and we are meant to listen to it.

My little nephew, in his childlike preciousness, was just doing what all of us *should* be doing: thinking of important life-and-death matters, the most significant one being "What will happen when I die?" It should not be considered a morbid topic, but one of utmost importance.

God is declaring that it is not good to live in denial of death. We are usually so busy in our daily routine of living that we don't give dying a second thought, but a frightened four-year-old was facing the inevitable facts. I kept thinking about him, *Little one, if only you knew how much God loves you! God loves you so much he sent His own Son to earth to show you that love.* Even at that young age, I knew my nephew could know with certainty God's love in an instant if he would just simply invite Jesus to come live in his heart.

Jesus came here specifically to tell all of us that God loves us and that we can be in heaven with Him only if we know Him personally and are free of sin that stands in the way of a close relationship. We must *all* humble ourselves and accept what Jesus did on the cross for us—every one of us. Only then will we be at peace, knowing with confidence where we will be when we die.

Waiting until tomorrow to make that important step of faith may be too late. We never know when our lives on this earth will end. We need to be prepared and think more like a fearful, but inquisitive and insightful, child while there is still time.

July 1997

13

No Coincidence, a God-Incidence

It was the night of October 8 at 9:00 p.m. when my nineteen-year-old daughter, Kim, came rushing into the house, frantically calling my name. She was talking fast, nervously, and between breaths she managed to relay what she had just experienced on the freeway coming home from her college volleyball game that night.

She gasped, "I was going about sixty-five miles per hour when another car merged onto the freeway and unexpectedly cut right in front of me!" Proceeding, she explained, "I cranked the wheel quickly to avoid hitting it" (which caused her car to swerve back and forth, out of control). "I tried to steady it," she added, "but no matter what I did, I couldn't get the car under control."

Kim veered straight across the five-lane freeway, heading toward the center divider. At the last minute she turned the wheel abruptly, barely missing the divider, and ended up coming to a stop in the carpool lane directly *facing* oncoming traffic. Panicked, she looked up, expecting an onslaught of cars because the place she was sitting was known to be one of the most heavily trafficked freeway locations in the state of California.

"Mom," she said in amazement, "when I looked up, there were no cars coming! There were no cars around at all!" Greatly relieved, but shaken, she managed to straighten the car out in the right direction and headed safely home.

The first words out of my mouth upon hearing of Kim's good fortune in this nearly disastrous potential accident were "Kim, you must have an angel sitting on your shoulder!" To have gone through this ordeal unscathed with no damage to herself or her car was truly a miracle. I have lived in this area for twenty-three years and have driven that same busy section of freeway many times. I can't recall ever seeing "no cars," or even a slight lull in the traffic there, in all that time. My second comment to Kim that night was "God must want you around a lot longer."

That sentiment was reaffirmed when a couple days later Kim received a letter from her grandfather. It was a surprise to hear from him, as he was not in the habit of writing letters to her. It was dated October 8, the day of the potential accident, which he knew nothing about, meaning that he wrote it and sent it before anything happened.

> To my Wonderful Grandchildren, Kim and Kevin,
>
> Do you know how much your grandpa loves you? Well, if you could look into my heart you would see that it is filled to the top. I have a great big heart, so you see I love you big, much, and a whole lot more! You know every time you pick up a newspaper you see where someone is badly injured or are a fatality either by some irresponsible driver or driving under the influence. Please forgive me. I am not lecturing or anything. I just want you to know how much I love you, and I want you around for a long, long, time. So be careful when you drive or are riding with someone else. Tell them to slow down and be ever so careful. You know I have found that you not only have to drive your car, but you have to drive everybody else's car, too. Forgive me, kids, you may not believe this, but the Lord brought this to my attention and I had to tell you this and how much I love you and want you around to love.
>
> Sincerely,
> Your Grandpa

After reading this letter, I felt certain that Kim did indeed have an angel sitting on her shoulder. I strongly believe that that angel was spurred into action by a dedicated, caring prayer warrior, her grandfather, who has told me that he prays for our family every day and could sense, in this situation, real trouble ahead.

I praise You, God, that Your spirit messengers of love protected our beautiful daughter Kim. I praise You for giving her a loving grandfather who interceded, at just the right moment, on her behalf.

October 1997

14

WHAT GOD SAYS ABOUT THE POOR

It had been a busy day at school, and I was hurriedly trying to get dinner ready before George got home. I almost didn't answer the phone when it rang, but I found myself picking up the receiver and saying a quick "Hello." I should have known. It was another request for money. It seemed I was constantly getting either calls or mail solicitations from just about every charitable organization. Rather annoyed, I responded, "No, I cannot help right now, and would you please stop calling me!"

Immediately, after hanging up, I felt sorry for being so abrupt. As I continued making dinner that night, I thought about the past few days. Hadn't our family gone out to celebrate joint birthday dinners and spent quite a bit on just that one meal? Kim had offhandedly mentioned the jeans she was wearing cost $150. Hadn't we been looking at buying earrings for me that cost $430? Recently we had remodeled our house for $55,000 and bought a new car for $35,000. We had been blessed with much, and I couldn't help but juxtapose that realization with all the hurting people in need here in the United States and all over the world.

Actually, the plight of the impoverished and poor had been bothering me more and more. As I read God's Word, it was becoming ever so clear how God felt about the poor and how He wanted *us* to feel about them. It was obvious they were not to be neglected. There were numerous Scriptures pertaining to the poor; they couldn't easily be dismissed. When Paul and Barnabas met with the pillars of the church—James,

Peter, and John—they discussed their respective calling to both Jews and non-Jews, and the only thing they specifically mentioned that they all needed to do was "remember the poor."[1]

Weren't some of God's greatest commandments to *"love your neighbor as yourself,"*[2] *"consider the helpless,"*[3] and be *"zealous for good deeds"*[4]? That struck right at the heart! Wouldn't God want us to think of others before self and forgo frivolous pleasures to make sure others less fortunate had their basic needs met? God did not merely mention the poor and needy a few times in His Word; there are many references in the Old and New Testaments exhorting us to be concerned for their welfare. Over the years, I collected some of these verses as I read through the Bible (NASB). Here are just a few of them:

> *The Lord your God ... executes justice for the orphan and the widow, and shows His love for the alien by giving him food and clothing. So show your love for the alien, for you were aliens in the land of Egypt.* (Deuteronomy 10:18–19)

> *The generous man will be prosperous and he who waters will himself be watered.* (Proverbs 11:25)

> *He who mocks the poor, taunts His Maker.* (Proverbs 17:5)

> *One who is gracious to a poor man lends to the Lord, and He will repay him for his good deed.* (Proverbs 19:17)

> *He who shuts his ear to the cry of the poor will also cry himself and not be answered.* (Proverbs 21:13)

> *Is it not to divide your bread with the hungry and bring the homeless poor into the house; when you see the naked, to cover him?* (Isaiah 58:7)

> *And if you give yourself to the hungry and satisfy the desire of the afflicted, then your light will rise in darkness and your gloom will become like midday.* (Isaiah 58:10)

For I was hungry, and you gave Me something to eat; I was thirsty and you gave Me something to drink; I was a stranger, and you invited Me in ... to the extent that you did it to one of these brothers of Mine, even the least of them, you did it to Me. (Matthew 25:35–40)

Give and it will be given to you ... for by your standard of measure it will be measured to you in return. (Luke 6:38)

Each one must do just as he has purposed in his heart, not grudgingly or under compulsion, for God loves a cheerful giver. (2 Corinthians 9:7)

He who steals must steal no longer; but rather he must labor, performing with his own hands what is good, so that he will have something to share with one who has need. (Ephesians 4:28)

Instruct them to do good, to be rich in good works, to be generous and ready to share. (1 Timothy 6:18)

But whoever has the world's goods, and sees his brother in need and closes his heart against him, how does the love of God abide in him? (1 John 3:17)

When Paul sadly was leaving the elders of the Church of Ephesus for the last time, the one thing he emphasized was to be a constant example in helping the poor by remembering the words of Jesus, "*It is more blessed to give than to receive.*"[5] He wanted to encourage them to follow Christ's example in always caring for the less fortunate.

Thinking of the helpless and helping the poor was not just a suggestion or reminder that God gave. It is obvious that this command to help the needy is extremely important. God wants us to not only *think* of the poor but also to focus on what we can *do* to turn our compassion into action.

Lord, give me a heart like Paul's to think of others more than myself, to be caring and willing to give. I know that at any point in time, the tables could be turned and I could be that desperate one in need. Direct me in ways in which I can care for the poor personally. This life is all about loving You, Lord, and loving others; it's not about me.

January 1998

15

God's Cleansing Power

While sitting at the kitchen table one morning in our Mammoth Mountain cabin, I was captivated by the white winter wonderland unfolding in front of me through the large picture window. I couldn't help but feel the wonder at God's creative design for our world. I was also noticing the contrasting dichotomy between winter's brown emptiness and the white refreshment of snow. It made me reflect on the analogy in our lives: our choice of living stagnant, sinful, dead lives *or* empowered, forgiven, fully alive ones. "God's Cleansing Power," the poem that I wrote that day, attempts to capture that stark polarity.

God tells us, "*... now is the Day of Salvation*"[1] and "*behold I make all things new.*"[2] Darkness turns to light, despair to hope, and death to life.

God's Cleansing Power

> Stirring reminders of God's cleansing power
> glimpsed in the beauty around us each hour:
> white glistening snow on stark, lifeless fronds;
> fresh rivers rushing that stir stagnant ponds;
> warm golden sunrises, ending cold nights;
> loving arms ridding a small child's fright;
> rainstorms reviving a thirsty dry land;
> strong stepping stones set in soft sinking sand.

God's Cleansing Power

Rebirths, beginnings … life is renewed.
Vivid examples of what God can do.
Through His Son, God makes our brokenness whole.
Dying for us, Christ restores our lost souls.
His Words of comfort bring solace to pain.
Lives are made holy that once were sin-stained.
Praise to our Lord, who gives life so complete.
In His forgiveness is beauty replete.

He sends the snow in all its lovely whiteness and scatters the frost upon the ground, and hurls the hail upon the earth. Who can stand before his freezing cold? But then he calls for warmer weather, and the spring winds blow and all river ice is broken. (Psalm 147:16–18 LB)

February 1998

16

A Prayer for My Children

Lord, as you know, I'm forty-eight now and at that point called midlife. It's true that this is an introspective time. I certainly have been doing a lot of thinking lately. I can see that the many chapters of my life as an actively-involved mother are slowly coming to an end. Kim is off to college, and Kevin is eighteen, living at home but definitely his own person, wanting and needing to be independent. Katie still has a few more years with us, which will help make this difficult transition easier.

As the time fleets by, I reflect on the past and a lump comes to my throat. There are so many wonderful memories, and yet I know another exciting phase is just beginning. My biggest anguish comes in my self-evaluation as a mother: Have I done my job giving my precious children that solid foundation they will need for the many ups and downs ahead? Mainly, did I do all that I could in helping to guide them toward developing a meaningful personal relationship with You?

Since You have heard from me many times on their behalf, I think You already know that my deepest desire is that they put You first in their lives above all else. My continual prayer is that they love You with all their heart, soul, mind, and strength. As a mother, I have tried to supply all their basic needs, but Lord, there is one need that only

A Prayer for My Children

You can supply. You can put the desire in their hearts to seek You, find You, and live foremost for You.

Lord, help my children to disentangle themselves from all the preoccupations and din of this world so they can see just You standing there with Your arms open wide, hearing You call their names. Increase their desire to study Your Word and to pray. Guide their footsteps so that they may not be conformed to this world but transformed in Your image. I know that with Your help, they will be kind and compassionate in their interactions with others and be humbled in their self-assessment. Please protect them from the Evil One, for the temptations in this world are many and the entrapments subtle. Eliminate any clouds of doubt so they may freely trust You to direct their paths.

I know You are always reaching out to them with love. Help them to see their need of You and realize that the only way to fill the void in their hearts is with the one who put it there. Help them to know that Your love is constant no matter what happens in their lives. You made them unique individuals, each a special design—valuable, purposeful, and significant. May their lives bring You honor. To that end, I know my role as a mother will be fulfilled and I will beam down from heaven with joy when my earthly days are ended. Amen!

March 1998

17

AM I A CHRISTIAN?

Our family was on vacation one Easter Sunday, and not wanting to miss church on this important day, we all piled into the car to attend the main service of a church near where we were staying. During the sermon, the pastor reviewed the agonizing and tortuous death of Jesus on the cross. He explained that Jesus was whipped, made to wear a scarlet robe and crown of long thorns, mocked and spat upon by the soldiers, and beaten unmercifully. To indicate the extent of the torture, our minister went into great detail about what happens to the body when experiencing death by crucifixion, and in essence, what pain Christ endured for us.

My mind began to wander momentarily. I was so happy that my family was all together and it was such a beautiful day. Easter was such a wonderful reason to celebrate. I rejoined the sermon just in time for the pastor to dogmatically comment, "If this doesn't affect you (referring to his lengthy description of Christ's crucifixion), then you must not be a Christian!"

I was so stunned! I looked around, wondering if that statement had affected others as it had affected me. Since when was a person's reaction to something the basis of his or her relationship with God, and when did it become the criterion for determining whether a person is a true Christian or not? This minister was an excellent Bible teacher and was also a well-read Christian author. The church building was large, with many individuals in the congregation. It was obvious he had quite a following. How could he so easily fall into the trap of legalism?

AM I A CHRISTIAN?

From what I knew, being a Christian had nothing to do with emotionalism or lack of it, whether I was a Democrat or Republican, whether I read the King James Version or *The Living Bible*, or whether I liked one kind of music or another. My faith was not based on what church I attended, how often I attended, whether I attended Sunday School or the church service, or whether I was a church member or not. Everything that I had ever read in the Bible indicated to me that being a Christian dealt exclusively with having faith and believing in the gospel message that I am a sinner made acceptable to God by the saving grace of His Son, Jesus Christ. I certainly was not going to lose my Christian status by my failures (such as not reacting the way another person thought I should), because I didn't gain it by my performance. We aren't Christians because of what we *do* or who we *are* (thank goodness), but because of what *God* did and who *He* is! Praise God!

God looks at what is in our heart, not at our outward appearances. My Lord's joy is in those who reverence Him,[1] as the psalmist said. There is no ready formula for each of us to follow to develop that reverent devotion that God so desires from us. Do we follow God's great command—to love Him with our hearts, minds, souls, and strength, and to love our neighbors as ourselves?[2] God has made all of us uniquely different, and how we praise and honor Him will vary. God is not looking at the externals, but at our hearts and at the resulting fruit that will bring Him glory.

Each of us must constantly reflect on what's important in the church and anywhere. As Paul accurately stated, *"We are made right with God by placing our faith in Jesus Christ."*[3] That's all that matters, and that's what makes one a Christian. Amen! And again I say, Amen!

Lord, I want to lift up Your name always. With Your Holy Spirit to guide me, help me to discern Your truth as I come to know you better through Scripture and as I pray. I love you so much. Continue to use me for Your glory!

April 1998

18

I'M RIGHT HERE

I had been listening to a radio program about a young mother with cancer who was going through chemotherapy. This exhausted mother was so frustrated and depressed because she was not able to do her normal activities. The radio minister offered these words of encouragement: "Relax. God is as close to you right now as He will ever be. Quit striving, and let Him love you. Give your body and emotions a chance to restore themselves."

I started thinking how hard it would be to have zero energy ... so sapped of vitality that it would be a struggle even to pray. It would be difficult to be the dependent one when you were used to being the organizer and director. You might be in such a state of anxiety and weariness that you wouldn't be able to feel God's presence at all. You might even begin to question if He really cared.

What would God's reaction to this doubt be? After reading Matthew 11:28–30, I created the following song, "Come to Me," showing what I imagined our loving and compassionate Lord of Life would say to any child of His who is suffering:

Come to Me

> Come to Me, all *you* who are weary.
> Come to Me, all *you* who need rest.
> Come to me, all *you* who are burdened.
> Yes, you will feel My gentleness.

I'm Right Here

> I am near and never will leave you.
> I'm as close as I'll ever be.
> Come to Me, and just let Me love you.
> Take My yoke and learn from Me.
>
> I'll be the strong one in your weakness.
> Lean on Me for the long, hard fight.
> I will lead you through the darkness.
> Come to Me; My burden is light.
>
> When you raise your arms, I will lift you.
> When you cry out, I will draw near.
> When you're on your knees, I will hear you.
> Come to Me; I'm always right here.

I would sit down at the piano and play the melody occasionally, but then I put the song in my notebook of original compositions for safekeeping. Out of sight, it was soon out of mind.

Not more than a month later, my sister, Nancy, contacted me to inform me that she would be having a lumpectomy. Soon after that, she got the surprising news that it was malignant and she would be undergoing surgery. With the results of that came even more unexpected news—cancer cells had been found in her lymph nodes, and she would need chemotherapy and radiation.

To my dismay, my energetic, nonstop sister was to become that frustrated, disheartened mother with cancer I had heard on the radio. Did God know that was going to happen? Of course He did! The Bible says He charts the path ahead for each one of us and tells us where to stop and rest.[1] He both precedes and follows each of us.[2]

Did I write those verses especially for my very own sister? Deep down I felt God had put that song in my heart for a special reason, and so I sent her a copy. God wanted Nancy to know that He would not be far away from her at any time. He would carry her in her weakness, hold her tenderly, and love her through the entire painful and exhausting ordeal. I felt God wanted to let her know that He would be as close as He would ever be, even when she would cry out in doubt, "Where are you, God?"

I know my Lord would tell her, "Nancy, I am right here ... and I always will be. Listen to my words and trust me."

Heavenly Father, please help Nancy feel Your presence and Your peace.

May 1998

19
WAIT AND HE WILL HELP YOU

My sister, Nancy, has been dealing with cancer the last seven months, undergoing chemotherapy and trying to remain positive and strong throughout the whole ordeal. All of our family and many friends have been supporting her, and many people have been praying for her. Knowing this, she has sometimes said, "If the power of prayer can heal, then I should be completely well!"

However, each time she returns from the doctors and receives the latest prognosis, there seems to be more complications. One time when I told her again that I was praying for her, in exasperation she asked, "Well, if God is there, why isn't He listening?" What does one say to that? What words of comfort can be given to ease the worry, the pain, and fear?

The next letter she wrote brought more of the same painful news:

> Well, my cancer count is up. I am not sure yet what it means. It could be a reaction to the new chemicals in the taxol, or it could mean cancer somewhere else in my body. I'm hanging in there. I've got to say, I am getting tired of all of this! The blood tests and shots hurt now because my veins are so tough and the needles are so fat in order to let fluids through. I cried at my last chemo session. My toes are totally numb and will remain so for several months.

When someone you love very much is hurting that badly, you are at a complete loss as to what to say or do. I kept Nancy in my thoughts and prayers, but it was not until the next morning, when I was quietly reading my Bible, that I felt God was pointing something out to me. The passage from Psalm 25:15–20 (LB) stated, *"My eyes are ever looking to the Lord for help, for he alone can rescue me. Come, Lord, and show me your mercy, for I am helpless and overwhelmed. In deep distress, my problems go from bad to worse. Oh, save me from them all! See my sorrows; feel my pain; forgive my sins ... let it never be said that I trusted you in vain!"*

Was that Nancy or David talking? David's plea to the Lord to save him from his enemies was just like Nancy's plea to God in her fight against her enemy, cancer. Each day as I continue to read small sections of Psalms, I am struck with David's deep distress and his total reliance on God to protect and save him. His words in Psalms (LB) are a comfort and encouragement for anyone going through difficult times.

> *Don't be impatient. Wait for the Lord, and He will come and save you! Be brave, stouthearted, and courageous. Yes, wait and he will help you.* (27:14)

> *O my soul, don't be discouraged. Don't be upset. Expect God to act! For I know that I shall again have plenty of reasons to praise him for all that he will do. He is my help! He is my God!* (42:11)

> *O my soul, why be so gloomy and discouraged? Trust in God! I shall again praise him for his wondrous help; He will make me smile again, for he is my God!* (43:5)

I sent my sister these Scriptures from Psalms hoping that she would cling tightly to them during the rest of this rough and frightening ordeal.

Nancy, you are in God's hands. Wait and trust! I will continue to pray for you with everything in me.

Lord, please keep her safe and at peace.

January 1999

Afterword:

Nancy did wait and trust, and she was pronounced cancer-free. For the last fifteen years, she has been faithfully serving God. Nancy is presently involved in prison ministry.

20

OPEN HEARTS ENTER

It was summer again, and I was involved in my third small-group summer Bible study. I always looked forward to this class because I had more time to read and study the Bible passages when I was not teaching. The questions about the lessons always pushed us to look at Scripture in more depth, and I was continually amazed at the important treasures that were buried in the pages that I had not noticed before.

Something that I was beginning to grasp for the first time as we studied the book of Mark was the length of time it took even Jesus' disciples to truly understand exactly who He was and what He could do. They traveled with Him, witnessing the many miracles He performed, and yet they continued to doubt and question. They saw the people flock to Him as He healed the sick, the dying, the lame, the blind, and the demon possessed. He rebuked the wind and calmed the sea. He fed five thousand people with five loaves of bread and two fish, and had twelve baskets full of scraps left over. The next day, His disciples saw Him walk on water and were astonished. *"They just sat there and were unable to take it in! They still didn't realize who he was even after the miracle the evening before! For they didn't want to believe!"*[1]

It was amazing to think that even after all this evidence of the deity of Jesus, His own disciples were not convinced of who was standing right in front of them. Were they all that fearful and hard-hearted? How could they be that blind after witnessing firsthand His power and glory? Even Jesus wondered, *"Can't you understand? Are your hearts too hard to take it in? Your eyes are to see with - why don't you look? Why don't you open your ears and listen?"* [2]

I was astounded that *"not even His brothers were believing in Him"* [3]

As I shook my head in silent condemnation, it suddenly struck me. Hadn't I been that same way for many years myself? Hadn't I acted similarly, not believing God was real and could work His miracles right after meeting a need in my life? Hadn't there been times when I knew God had spoken to me through His Word or circumstances, or through other Christians, but then, within a few days, I was doubting and questioning not only God's ability but also His very existence?

I kept reading the Bible and praying, open to learning, seeking answers, and desiring to know Truth. When I finally came to the end of myself and in faith surrendered my life to Christ, that's when my new life began.

Looking back, now fourteen years later, I can see that my life *has* changed. It's never been the same since then, and it will never be the same again. My number-one desire in life is to please God. I'm always looking for ways to serve Him. Now, with the help of the Holy Spirit, I understand the Bible, which had always proved difficult in the past. Just as the Scriptures say, *"I was blind, but now I see."* [4]

It was a long journey to finally understanding, but Jesus never gave up on me. And He promises all of us: *"seek and you will find; knock, and it will be opened to you."* [5]

Lord, I have learned firsthand that You will never close the door if our hearts are open. I pray that all people everywhere will come to know that truth for themselves.

July 1999

21

IN AN INSTANT

The teenage son of some friends of ours had been in jail several weeks, waiting for his preliminary hearing. In that short time, the father of this boy relayed to us that "he had become quite religious" and was now participating in a Bible study. I was very excited to hear this news, for I knew that if anything can miraculously turn a life around, it is developing a personal relationship with Jesus Christ.

Commenting on this sudden change, one of our other friends, who also knew the family, remarked rather cynically, "I guess Davey got himself a case of instant religion!" He was skeptical that an enlightened transformation of that magnitude could occur so quickly and be genuine. It was a view that I had heard expressed often before—that Christianity is just a quick short-term fix for being down-and-out; a contrived opiate for the desperate that can't possibly be real.

Ironic, isn't it? That's just the point. At the end of our rope is exactly where God wants us to be! Only then can we see our insufficiency to handle everything on our own. Only then are we in proper alignment with God: humbled, broken, and dependent on a loving, forgiving Savior. From outward appearance, it seems that people turn to God only when they have nowhere else to go—because it is true. And we don't need to wait until we are sitting in prison for that decision to be made.

Many cynics have difficulty believing that God can so instantly come into a person's life, especially a sinful life, because they hold to the theory that our relationship with God is based on our performance. However, as Romans 3:23 states, *"all have sinned and fall short of the glory of God"*[1] and *"there is none righteous, no not even one."*[2] It is our nature to be self-focused, self-absorbed, and sinful. All of us are lost and on the road to destruction, and yet there are those who want to believe that they are innately good and don't need to be saved. That's why God sometimes allows us to endure those trials and tribulations, such as being incarcerated—so that we become broken and acknowledge our need for God's help.

We can ask for God to come into our lives at any moment, and the conversion *can* happen in an instant. All of us know people who have made a change overnight because they met almighty God personally. Nothing they could have concocted could have made such a dramatic and permanent change in their attitude and behavior. One of the greatest examples in history is the Roman soldier, Saul, whose life's mission changed from killing Christians to becoming a devoted disciple of Jesus after his conversion on the road to Damascus. *"Instantly, it was as though scales fell from his eyes. Paul could see, and was immediately baptized."*[3]

Paul's life and writings attest to the reality and permanence of the change. He began preaching the good news that Jesus, whom he used to persecute, was the Son of God. *"All who heard him were amazed ..."*[4] because of the change. This was more than a contrived opiate for the desperate. Christ's Spirit was now living in Him carrying out God's Will, and Paul would never be the same again.

We can all find that same truth just as instantly when we take our eyes off ourselves and with great humility look into the loving eyes of our Savior: *"all are saved the same way, by the free gift of the Lord Jesus."*[5] It can take place in a prison cell, on our deathbed in a hospital, at church, in the confines of our own home, or anywhere. We just need to pray this simple prayer:

God, forgive me. I know I am a sinner. I know I cannot get into heaven on my own. I accept You as my personal Savior. I believe you died on the cross for me. Thank you for forgiving me. Thank you for loving me. Amen.

July 1999

22

JOHN HAS HODGKIN'S DISEASE

I had just received a very upsetting call from one of my best friends that her husband, John (only forty-three years old), had just been diagnosed with Hodgkin's disease. The biopsy indicated that he had progressed to stage four, which meant that the disease had already spread considerably through his bone marrow. Things didn't look good. John began chemotherapy right away.

How could I help? The only thing I could do was pray and try to send him encouraging messages. What could I say? I was trying to think of a Bible verse that he could hang on to, but which one? I just couldn't come up with the right one, so I decided to read one of my favorites—Proverbs 3:5–6 (NASB):

> *Trust in the Lord with all you heart*
> *And do not lean on your own understanding.*
> *In all your ways acknowledge Him*
> *And He will make your paths straight.*

For some reason I continued to read on, and there it was! Proverbs 3:8: *"It shall be health to thy navel and marrow to thy bones."*

I had never noticed that verse before, but it was so perfect for John. Obviously, God wanted him to hear it. God knew the right verse all along, and I was so glad He led me to find it. Truly, God's Word is *"living and powerful."*[1] As Jesus Himself stated, " … *the words that I have spoken to you are spirit and are life."*[2]

John Has Hodgkin's Disease

I quickly sent the Proverbs Scripture to John. Later, my friend mentioned several times how this very pertinent passage had encouraged both of them through a very painful and difficult journey.

Heavenly Father, You gave us new lives through Jesus Christ so that we could help and serve others. May You continue to reveal Yourself to us, and may we see clearly each day how Your will can be done.

Months later, John's last test indicated no sign of the disease. I praise God!

November 1999

23

LETTER TO CECIL ON MY FIFTIETH

This is a letter I wrote to my father-in-law on my fiftieth birthday.

March 14, 2000

Dear Cecil,

Hello! How are you today? Well, this is my official fiftieth landmark day! It doesn't seem possible, but it is true! I thought I'd type you a note before the activities of the day begin.

When you were here last Sunday, you asked me if I was happy. I didn't say, at that time, what was foremost on my mind, but I decided to tell you now. On my birthday, or any other day, my greatest joy is knowing my Savior, Jesus Christ, and His unconditional love for me. I want to know Him more all the time and try to read the Bible daily (which is easier right now because I'm on my intersession break from school). I love to get up in the morning when it is still quiet and have some private time reading and praying. I listen to Christian music all the time and can't seem to get enough.

Letter to Cecil on My Fiftieth

My prayers always include all the people I love so much. It is my earnest plea that all my family and friends come to know Jesus as their personal Savior. If they could only know how awesome and real this relationship could be! If they would just break down the wall of pride and realize their great need of His grace and love. Christ would be there with open arms, as He always is. He is so patient.

I know I cannot make that reality happen for others, but I wish I could convey to them the peace, beauty, fulfillment, and hope that comes with the emptying of self and the filling of God Himself. I received so many wonderful gifts for my fiftieth, but the greatest birthday gift would be knowing with certainty that all my family and friends will be saved. I love you, Eva [my mother-in-law], and Debbie [George's sister who lives with them] very much. I have been blessed with our family ties. My prayer is that we will all be eternally tied together.

I've got to get ready for the rest of the day, and off to my students! May God continue to bless and keep you. You are very special to me.

Love,
Barbara

24

HOW CAN I HELP?

As I continue my daily journey reading through the Bible, I can't help but notice how often the instruction to take care of the poor, the helpless, and the needy is given. If God has brought up this subject so many times, there must be a reason. More often lately, I have been asking myself, "What am I doing to follow God's directives to help the downtrodden, the homeless, and the lonely?"

I reflected on the past. I *had* attempted to do my part by giving our family's discards to deserving organizations that would distribute them to the needy. I *had* participated in our church's yearly outreach day to the neighboring community. Along with my regular tithe to the church, occasionally I *had* added that extra amount in the collection plate for the special monthly collection taken for those in dire circumstances and need.

There were other things I had done to help the needy, but somehow all of this seemed very little, only futile noble attempts, after reading about the numerous Biblical accounts of the compassion and love that permeated the life of Jesus wherever He went. He had such a heart for the poor, the sick, and the needy. I wanted to do more, but what? Teaching full-time, being involved in all the family activities, and working to complete my master's degree left me little time to do all that I felt I needed to do to follow Jesus' example.

I thought, *Maybe I can work in a soup kitchen.* I even called a few numbers to investigate this possibility, which resulted in a dead end. Actually, I reflected that maybe this particular involvement wasn't me anyway, since I didn't really relish the drudgery of preparing meals and working in my own kitchen these harried days.

It's interesting that God has a way of oftentimes presenting answers in the most unexpected moments. I was just driving down the main street of town, doing my usual errands, and had stopped at a light. I was absorbed in thought, listening to the radio, when a movement up ahead and to my left caught my attention. A man was adeptly turning the wheels of his wheelchair as he made his way across the street, coming toward my corner. It was readily apparent that he had no legs from about the knees down. He appeared to be about my age, so I surmised that his disability probably resulted from the Vietnam War. He was able to move very capably, but my heart suddenly just went out to him. Filled with compassion, I just sent a little prayer up to God: "Lord, bless this man."

As he swiftly came past me, he turned with a big smile, pointed to my ten-year-old car, and gave me a thumbs up! It was such an unexpected action, and I gave him the biggest smile. He kept looking back at me with a big grin the whole time he crossed the street. It seemed as if we had connected in some way and it was making both of us smile inside and out.

For some reason, I keep thinking back to that incident, and I am now realizing that maybe God is telling me something. I can pray for people anytime and anywhere, and God listens. Maybe that is one of the best ways to help. It doesn't have to be a long, formal prayer in the privacy of our homes, or corporate prayer in a large group. It can be quick impromptu pleadings for anyone, such as the hurting mother I had just read about in the newspaper that morning who was grief-stricken with the loss of her twenty-four-year-old daughter who had been hit by a drunk driver and burned by the fiery car explosion. I had prayed, "God, help this mother make it through another day. May she find Your peace and Your will to go on."

There is a wonderful man who is head of the music ministry at our church and lives near our home. He has mentioned that he often says a little prayer for our family as he drives by. That has been such a blessing once I learned about it. Why couldn't I do this too, in just the little everyday happenings?

Recently, I had read this quote by Max Lucado: "The sign of the saved is their love for the least."[1] It made me think of the words of Jesus: *"Truly I tell you, whatever you did for one of the least of these brothers and sisters of mine you did for me."*[2] God has given all of us eyes to see the hurt all around us and a heart to do something about it.

Lord, help me to see the need of those around me. I want to be Your humble servant. If a little prayer is needed, remind me to take time to speak to You on their behalf. I want to be obedient to Your will for the lives of others.

August 2000

25

IN HIS HEAD, NOT HIS HEART

It was a September day when George and I were having a discussion about points made in our Sunday school class. It was often repeated each Sunday how important a personal relationship with Jesus Christ was to a person's life and salvation. George casually said, "I tried it, and it didn't work." Not being sure what he meant, I queried, "What do you mean?" He stated he had accepted Christ and nothing had happened.

I was ecstatic to hear that news. For so many years, I had been praying that George would know Christ personally. I knew how much my life had changed once I accepted Christ; I began hungering to read the Bible and know Jesus better, and desiring to be used by God and to worship Him. It was obvious that George was seeking answers, because he was attending church more regularly than before and was more receptive to learning and to growing spiritually. Plus, George acted more Christianlike than many people I knew who professed to be Christian. He was a man of integrity—honest, generous, and caring. He was the most loving husband, son, and father.

He said he had accepted Christ, and scripturally, I knew that if George had humbly asked God for forgiveness, and believed with all his heart that Jesus died for him, then he was saved. I began to read through the Bible and find as many passages as I could that confirmed that truth:

> *If you believe that Jesus is the Christ - that he is God's Son and your Savior – then you are a child of God.* (1 John 5:1b LB)

Anyone who believes and says that Jesus is the Son of God has God living in him, and he is living with God. (1 John 4:15 LB)

For God so loved the world that he gave his only begotten Son that whoever believes in Him shall not perish, but have everlasting life. (John 3:16 NASB)

There were many more: 2 Chronicles 15:2; Psalm 9:10; Acts 10:43; John 1:12; 6:39–40, 47; 11:25–26; and Romans 10:13. I wrote all of these out for George and then added a personal note: "These all seem to say to me that if you have sincerely asked Christ to be your personal Savior and have done it for yourself (not me) and really need God in your life (and are not just trying it out), then you are saved." I suggested that he get to know God better by reading the Bible.

He read the note and thanked me, and we did not talk about it again until the next week on our way to Sunday school. I offhandedly suggested that with his father's eighty-fourth birthday approaching, I thought the best present he could give him was to tell him that he had accepted Christ as his personal Savior. George paused, pondered, and then hesitatingly said, "I believe in God and have accepted Him here (pointing to his head), but not here (indicating his heart)." There was not much I could say at that point. He was aware of the difference, understanding his need for unquestioning and total surrender, but he was not ready to relinquish complete control.

As I sat next to George in our class that morning, I had to admit that I was disappointed. I so wanted him to experience that same joy that I have in knowing and loving my Savior. However, I knew it was all in God's timing and I had to keep trusting God. He would know best when George was ready. I had seen him drawing closer to God over the years and was truly thankful that he was more receptive than in the past. George was in God's loving hands, and I just had to keep hoping and praying.

I was drawn out of my thoughts when I heard our Sunday school teacher saying something from the Bible about the heart. What was it? *"For it is by believing in his heart that a man becomes right with God."*[1]

In His Head, Not His Heart

He then proceeded to relate a story about a conversation he had had with a gentleman. This man understood everything; he knew he fell short of God's standard, he knew he was a sinner, he knew God had sent His Son to save him, he knew all about the gospel message, but he didn't believe it in his heart. Intellectually he understood, but he had not submitted his will, and that was the crucial step.

I sat almost frozen. God had definitely caught my attention. Was it having the same effect on George? Did George realize that God was speaking directly to him through the voice of our teacher? Our teacher continued to explain how, for over a year, the same thing happened with him as he listened and watched other Christians. He understood what was being said but hadn't accepted it in his heart. He finally acknowledged that he had heard enough; all that had been said to him was having an overwhelming effect on him. As he aptly expressed it, he "waved the white flag," gave up, and believed in his heart.

He then addressed the class, and said, "Some here may be the same way. You've heard this all before but are holding out."

Oh, George, are you listening? I wondered. *God is speaking personally to you.*

Our teacher continued, saying that it is a man's self-righteousness and pride that stand in the way of this close relationship. People think that they don't need God; that they can do it on their own. He ended that portion of the lecture by saying that we need to pray for those individuals who have heard it in their heads but have not submitted their wills.

Oh, Lord, help George to hear You. Break down those walls that keep him from You. He needs You. May he see clearly that You are reaching out to him. Thank You, Lord. You are an awesome God.

I have faith that someday George will know, without a doubt, that Jesus is Lord in his heart.

September 2000

26

A Daily Walk

For the last few months I have developed the daily habit of walking with my new friend Marsha. We both have found this practice to be invigorating and enjoyable. Walking regularly does take a fair amount of self-discipline, as does any form of exercise, especially after a long day at work. However, I'm finding that walking is already becoming somewhat habitual. Right around 5:00 p.m. every day, my legs and feet start fidgeting, anxious to get out in the fresh air and stride through the familiar neighborhood route. Even when other appointments interfere, Marsha and I do our best to work around those interruptions, adjusting times or shortening our regular three-mile course. We also keep each other accountable, for we don't like to let each other down. For both of us, walking has become of utmost importance, and we try to put it first, with other things taking second place.

An added benefit to physical exercise and clearing the mind is that I have gotten to know Marsha so much better. We have fifty minutes of uninterrupted time together and have become great sounding boards for one another. We are taking time to develop a meaningful relationship that becomes more special every day. I started thinking, *What if we transferred this same walking discipline over to developing our faith? Would we know God better?*

Oftentimes, people will admit they don't feel a close personal relationship with their heavenly Father. If we want to know the will of God, hear His voice, and see God working in our lives, might we try giving Him that same commitment of time and effort we would give walking? To cultivate that love relationship, we would need the same self-discipline, diligence, and dedication we might commit to a walking habit. We would need to set aside daily uninterrupted time to be with God, and make sure other activities came afterward. We would need to view giving God quality time every day for our spiritual growth as being as important as our regular time spent devoted to our physical well-being.

How well the disciple Timothy knew this principle when he said, *"Spend your time and energy in the exercise of keeping spiritually fit. Bodily exercise is all right, but spiritual exercise is much more important and is a tonic for all you do."*[1]

What would happen if we walked only once a week? That would be better than nothing, but we likely would not be in good physical condition. Also, our relationship with our walking partner would not be as close or meaningful. Likewise, going to church just once a week wouldn't dramatically change our spiritual growth; nor would our relationship with God be as close or meaningful. Just as with walking regularly, we could make this interaction with God so habitual that things just wouldn't feel right unless we personally connected every day.

What would those added benefits be if we approached God as our daily walking partner? We would be able to talk to Him every day, confide in Him, and allow Him to be our sounding board. We would learn all about Him as we trekked in the neighborhood of His Word. We would be taking the time to develop a meaningful relationship that would become more special every day.

Jesus made a deliberate effort to spend time with God. It would be advisable to let Him be our example. Very early in the morning, while it was still dark, Jesus got up, left the house, and went to a solitary place where he prayed.[2] He often withdrew to lonely places and prayed.[3] He regularly spent time in God's Word, reading in the synagogue or quoting Scripture. If Jesus, the Son of God, found time to spend precious time with His Father, should we not attempt to do the same?

Since God's whole purpose in creating us is for us to seek after Him and feel our way toward Him and find Him,[4] I think God would applaud any effort we made to structure our day to draw closer to Him. Wouldn't knowing God personally be the most important thing someone could do in his or her lifetime, even more so than daily physical exercise? I'm sure God would be saying, "Don't wait ... start your habit of walking with me today!"

Heavenly Father, You gave each of us a spirit not only of power and love but also of self-discipline.[5] May we lean on You to help us develop the habit of spending one-on-one time with You every day. You can be our walking partner for life (and even after!).

October 2000

27

THE LIGHT OF DAY

As I was driving through town today, I noticed a young man with a broad-brimmed hat standing on the corner holding a rather large sign. It read, "Evil's greatest foe is the Light of day." As I continued to drive home, I mulled that thought over. It took me back in time fourteen years ago, when I was just beginning to understand certain biblical truths, such as this one, through personal experience.

Back then, when I had turned my life over to Christ at the age of thirty-five, a rather bizarre occurrence was happening to me as I attempted to develop a closer relationship with God. Every time I tried to pray, all these foul words would jump in, making it impossible for me to concentrate and communicate with God. I couldn't understand what was happening, but it persisted. Not only was I thinking I must be a terrible person to allow this to happen, but I was also wondering why God was allowing this to happen. Was I going crazy?

Strangely enough, the next Tuesday, on my way to teach my *Kiddie-Gym* classes, I turned on the radio and stopped suddenly as a preacher with a Southern accent, whom I had never heard before (or since!), was talking. He explained how he had been praying the night before and "this little black, devilish-looking creature jumped right in front of him and blasphemed God and continued to say the most foul, awful things imaginable." The pastor said he started shouting for this thing to leave and saying that he wasn't going to listen to it. He preached that God would do something if He could, and that he knew how odd that must sound to the listening audience, for God is almighty and all-powerful and can do anything (*"I have been given all authority in heaven and on earth"*[1]). However, God gave us free wills and we can choose to listen to this blaspheme or cast it out.

I remember realizing then, for the first time in my life, the extent to which evil was trying to make headway into my life, instilling fear and doubt, trying to dissuade me from God and getting close to Him. This fact was further heightened as I read Paul's words in 1 Corinthians: *"Therefore I make known to you that no one speaking by the Spirit of God says, Jesus is accursed, and no one can say Jesus is Lord except by the Holy Spirit."*[2]

Coincidentally, at this time I was also reading a book in which the Christian author said that when some involuntary oath of cursing Christ comes out, there's an evil power behind it. That was exactly what was happening to me! I was a threat to the Enemy, and his strategic scheme of sabotage was set in motion. Satan abhorred my closeness to my Savior and was determined to destroy our newfound intimacy.

Respected Pastor Rick Warren explained this attempt to be undone by the enemy: "Sometimes while you are praying, Satan will suggest a bizarre or evil thought just to distract you and shame you. Don't be alarmed or ashamed by this, but realize that Satan fears your prayers and will try anything to stop them. Instead of condemning yourself with, 'How could I think such a thought?' treat it as a distraction from Satan and immediately refocus on God."[3]

Not only was I becoming more aware of evil's invasion into my own life and its plotting of my downfall, but I was also becoming more cognizant of just how pervasive this force was all around me. One such incident occurred as I walked into my house one day and my son was watching an episode of *Conan the Adventurer* on television. Conan was in the process of stabbing an opponent with a sword, and this vision literally jumped right out at me. It was so vivid, so real, and so evil. In the next couple of days, I observed my children watching other TV shows and movies with gremlins and other ugly little creatures in them, which negatively affected me as well. At that moment I wanted so much to protect and shelter my children from these evil influences that were not only being shown to me through the medium of television, but were also everywhere about, although many of them were not quite so obvious.

The Light of Day

I realized then that God had not deserted me. He was allowing me to experience evil, making me aware of its subtlety and insidiousness. He was telling me to be alert, recognize it, and resist it. As the Bible directs, *"Put on all of God's armor so that you will be able to stand safe against all strategies and tricks of Satan. For we are not fighting against people made of flesh and blood, but against persons without bodies - the evil rulers of the unseen world, those mighty satanic beings and great evil princes of darkness who rule this world; and against huge numbers of wicked spirits in the spirit world."*[4] In the thick of the battle, I would need to call on His name: "Jesus, help me!" He would fight the battle for me.

Satan's tactic is to cause us to become so conditioned to what is ugly, destructive, perverse, and evil that we won't recognize what it truly is when it is staring us in the face. We will no longer see those evil things as a threat, because over time, being exposed to it constantly, we will gradually wear down and become desensitized. Satan is a formidable enemy whom we must recognize and battle daily.

God was reassuring me that we would never be without His sufficiency. We would not be fighting this battle alone: *"... use every piece of God's armor to resist the enemy whenever he attacks, and when it is all over, you will still be standing up."*[5] Satan, who is the *"god of this world,"* wants to keep us blind so we are unable to see the *"light of the gospel"* shine into our hearts.[6] Jesus Christ, the enemy's greatest foe, is that glorious "Light of Day," the image of God shining in a dark world.

Lord, I know I must cling to You all the more, for You will help guard my heart and my mind and protect me from the Enemy.

> *The Lord is the stronghold of my life - of whom shall I be afraid? ... Though an army besiege me, my heart will not fear; though war break out against me, even then will I be confident.* (Psalm 27:1b–3 LB)

October 2000

28
Not Fitting In

Once more, it was bothering me that I just didn't feel as if I were fitting in. I was enjoying less and less what seemed to be top priority to so many other people. The TV, such a popular pastime for others, held no fascination for me with its main fare of dysfunctional families, affairs, violence, illicit sex, and commercialism. I had often enjoyed going out to the movies, but even that activity had become less appealing. Movies, plays, and even some musicals were offensive to me not only because of the sordid subject matter but also because I had to endure the Lord's name being maligned or degraded in several of them (actually, in almost all of them!). The newspaper, filled with life's worst, was becoming more difficult for me to read every day. Knowing that the computer had so quickly become an instrument of evil, with pornography being the number-one business associated with it, was equally upsetting. Shopping had even lost its attraction for me. Sometimes I could hardly stand being surrounded by so many things as I made my way past brimming counters and down crowded aisles, everything vying to be purchased to supposedly make my life better.

I began questioning myself more frequently. "What's wrong with me? Why don't I enjoy doing what so many people consider fun and important? Am I really such a stick-in-the-mud? I don't want to alienate my friends or family, and I want to enjoy being with them, but how can I when the desires of my heart are so different from theirs?"

Not Fitting In

It seems strange to say, but I was feeling lonely, and this did not happen just one or two times. I knew I wasn't really alone, as people were usually around me, but even so, I felt isolated, like an outsider.

A quote I had read somewhere came to mind: "If you walk with God, you'll be out-of-step with the world." How true that was for me. Jesus said that when we have His Holy Spirit within us, we will be in this world but will not feel a part of it. He knew only too well the feeling of isolation and estrangement.

Right about this time in my Bible study, we were examining Satan in depth. It was really opening my eyes to some important biblical truths about not fitting in. According to God's Word, if people are not with Christ, they are against Him.[1] They go along with the crowd and are just like all the others, obeying Satan, *"who is at work right now in the hearts of those who are against the Lord."*[2] Apostle John stated, *"We know that we are children of God and that all the rest of the world around us is under Satan's power and control."*[3] The goal of Satan, described in the Bible as *"the ruler of this world"*[4] and *"the god of this world,"*[5] is to keep unbelievers in bondage, influencing their activities, views, interests, and goals, and blinding them so they are unable to see the glorious light of His Word.

This new insight was helping me see things more clearly. It was most assuredly a blessing that I did *not* feel a part of things. Rather than bemoaning that I was a foreigner, a lonely sojourner in this world of ours, I needed to stop feeling sorry for myself and be ever so grateful. I realized that Satan would do anything and everything possible to halt the truth of Christ in the world, including planting seeds of discontent and discouragement in my mind and the minds of others like me who feel different from the crowd. I am so thankful that the veil of self-doubt was lifted from my eyes.

So what should my mind-set be, and how should I act as I continue to live in this world and interact with the people I live with, work with, and love? First of all, I think I need to face the fact that like Paul, because of Christ and the cross, *"my interest in all the attractive things of the world was killed long ago and the world's interest in me is also long dead."*[6]

Furthermore, I must not let the world, its wealth, its delights, its attractions, and its search for success crowd out God's message from my heart. Like apostle Paul in the Bible, *"I must put aside all else, counting it worth less than nothing, in order that I can have Christ, and become one with him ..."*[7] Of utmost importance, I must allow the Holy Spirit to control my life as I continue to immerse myself in God's Word and pray. I am certain that if I stay close to my Lord and Savior, He will tell me what to do.

As Pastor Rick Warren stated, "You will never feel completely satisfied on earth, because you were made for more. You will have happy moments here, but nothing compared with what God has planned for you. Life on earth is just a temporary assignment."[8] It is a life in which I may not fit in here, but I will live to please my Savior and prepare to fit into my heavenly home, my eternal happiness.

July 2001

29

THINGS ARE DIFFERENT NOW, OR ARE THEY?

It was spring, and our school was celebrating Grandparents' Day. I had asked all the grandparents attending to share something they remembered about school that was different from the way it is now. Many of them remembered going to one-room schoolhouses in which several grades were together in one classroom. Others mentioned that their classroom was not as colorful, had fewer resources, and had no technology. Some said that the teachers were stricter, didn't smile as much, and were more matronly. It was really fascinating hearing how things had changed in such a short period of time.

Later that evening, as I reflected on the day, I couldn't help but think about a story my mother had told me about her high school graduation. I was really thankful that the events of that occasion didn't occur nowadays.

The year was 1938. The nineteen seniors in her graduating class in Pennsylvania were going to visit Washington, DC, for the annual senior trip. These individuals had saved money all through high school for this special excursion. There was one black boy, Dwayne Davis, in the class. Everyone else was white. As the trip was being planned, it was discovered that because of Dwayne's skin color, he would have to stay in a different hotel than the other students. In addition, when taking any public transportation, he would have to be seated in a different section than all his classmates—one for blacks only. He would not be able to eat in the same restaurants as his friends. Even though this student had saved his money, was well-liked by his classmates and teachers, and was excited about this adventure like everyone else, he decided not to go.

I thought about how sad this must have been for him. I was sure that this memory would still be a painful one for him if he was still living today. Thinking about this made me recall something that occurred in my own town when I was growing up in 1960.

I remembered a black girl in my elementary school who was a year younger than me. She stood out mainly because she was the only black girl in the entire school. I remembered her quiet manner and how smart she was. She always dressed nicely and was very polite. I liked her a lot, and so did everyone else. Her parents both worked in education; her father was an administrator for our school district, and her mother was a teacher. This was a wonderful family, very cultured and well educated. However, even though they worked in my hometown and were contributing members, when it came to settling down there, they were not allowed to buy a house because of their skin color. They ended up purchasing a beautiful home in a nearby city, left the school district, and I never saw them again. What a hurtful message this sent (and it's hard to believe this was only forty-two years ago).

I was thinking, *I'm so glad everything is different now.* It was good knowing that people today were more civilized, less prejudiced. But then, I remembered an incident that occurred only seven years ago, when I was teaching at another school in my same district.

Our school had been asked to sing for a community organization that was having a luncheon, and since I had been teaching songs to the entire grade level every week, my principal asked if I would be willing to have the students perform. I was a bit reluctant, but I accepted. The students picked out some of their favorite songs: "Fifty Nifty United States," "We Salute the Presidents," "God Bless America," and "Dr. Martin Luther King." They were excited!

I vividly remember the day. There I was, guiding 110 fifth-grade students as they streamed along the neighborhood street over to a facility several blocks away. Many of these students, mostly Hispanic and some black, had never performed outside of school, so this was a new experience for them. As we arrived, the audience was already sitting at nicely decorated tables, patiently waiting as we lined ourselves up on stage. I could tell the students were nervous, but once we started singing, they relaxed.

We sang three of the songs to rousing applause. Then, we sang our last number, "Dr. Martin Luther King," a song the students always seemed to like. I distinctly recall that when we finished singing, there was very little applause. I recall feeling disappointed because this was a song I had written, and I was proud of it. Then, as we filed out of the hall, I noticed how quiet it was. I thought it was odd that there were no smiles or appreciative comments. A few minutes later, several students came up to me and said that some negative comments had been directed at them by several individuals in the audience about our last song: "Why did you pick that song?" and "Why did you sing a song about that man?"

I couldn't believe my ears! We were living in the nineties, during which there was so much talk of acceptance, tolerance, and equality, and yet there were obviously still remnants of racial prejudice lingering in the hearts of people right here (and others, I reasoned). I walked back to school with a new awareness of something that up to that point had been unfamiliar to me—discrimination. I was sorry that these students and I had witnessed it firsthand, especially when our motive was to do something positive in our community. I guess it wasn't surprising that no one came out after the program to thank us for coming, and I never received a thank-you note or a call expressing appreciation for our program.

I have never forgotten the feeling I had that day. I think that's all the more reason that I have such respect and admiration for Dr. Martin Luther King. He was such a fighter for justice and fairness, and yet he did it peacefully, with dignity and grace. Being a minister, he based his philosophy on the teachings of Christ; it was a philosophy in which a person's race, nationality, economic level, and social position were irrelevant.

Jesus was the perfect example of nondiscrimination. He daily interacted with numerous individuals from all walks of life and all races. He was seen with prostitutes and contemptible tax collectors. He embraced Jews and Gentiles, men and women, and welcomed conversations with kings and others in power, as well as those with little status. Jesus did not look at surface conditions and circumstances but looked at the heart.

Some of His disciples, like Paul, espoused this nondiscriminating attitude: *"There is neither Jew nor Greek, there is neither slave or free, there is neither male nor female; for you are all one in Christ."*[1] Apostle Peter testified to a change in his outlook through personal experience: *"You know it is against the Jewish laws for me to come into a Gentile home like this. But God has shown me in a vision that I should never think of anyone as inferior."*[2]

It is only too evident that pride and bitterness can destroy us. Jesus directed us to love and care for others, and that means relinquishing any ill will or prejudices of the past. We will never find peace if we allow resentment to reign in our souls. We all need to do more than talk about acceptance and love for it to become a reality.

Lord, we need Your help so we can be changed individuals. Fill us with Your unconditional love and forgiveness. Only then will we be able to say confidently without question, "Yes, things are different now."

April 2002

30

MY SPIRITUAL SACRIFICES

It was Easter, and our entire family was home for dinner and family togetherness. The TV had been on all afternoon, displaying "very important" basketball games. The food, which had taken a lot of time to prepare, was ready to be eaten, and I asked if we could turn the TV off. Unfortunately, there were still four minutes left of the game. This particular game had already been on for two and a half hours, and I knew that with numerous commercials (especially at the end of games), four minutes could easily stretch out to be half an hour. My request was met with much unhappiness from all the males in the group. Reluctantly, George turned the TV down, but not off. So while we stood in our traditional family circle, holding hands to say grace, the TV could still be heard in the background, and the action could still be observed.

I can remember feeling so put out afterward. I had planned on saying a portion of a prayer that Paul had spoken to the Ephesians in honor of Easter; I had even memorized it. But in my frustration, I totally blanked. So I never said these encouraging words of Paul's to everyone: May *"we see clearly and really understand who Christ is and all he has done for (us), and may our "hearts be flooded with light so that we can see something of the future that he has called us to share."*[1]

I thought to myself, rather cynically, that our hearts were certainly being flooded with light—the flashing pictures of the TV!

The next morning when I was doing my Bible study and having some quiet time, I just couldn't focus. I truly wanted to do what God commanded in His Word—have a thankful heart and be content in every circumstance[2]—but I just kept thinking about the day before and dwelling in my disappointment. Wasn't Easter a celebration of Christ's sacrifice for all of us? Shouldn't He get center stage? I was definitely feeling squelched and sorry for myself. Satan was certainly having a field day with my emotions, and even though I knew that, I was still having a hard time letting go of my discouragement.

So, as I sat at my desk, I started out with more of an emotional plea to God—no thanksgiving, no praises. Then I opened my *Living Bible* and for some reason started reading portions of Luke. God always has a way of getting right to the heart of the matter (and not always what we want to hear!). Luke 12:51–53 (LB) states, *"Do you think I have come to give peace to the earth? No! Rather, strife and division! From now on families will be split apart, three in favor of me, and two against – or perhaps the other way around. A father will decide one way about me; his son the other; mother and daughter will disagree ..."*

Okay, Lord, I can see the reality of that all too clearly, but how can I bear it when I love my family so much and don't want anything to separate us? How many times have I prayed that we would be united in making You a priority? Please help me know what to do.

The very next passage I read was Luke 14:26–27: *"Anyone who wants to be my follower must love me far more than he does his own father, mother, wife, children, brothers, or sisters – yes, more than his life – otherwise he cannot be my disciple. And no one can be my disciple who does not carry his own cross and follow me."*

I started thinking, *What does it mean to carry my own cross?* Christ carried His cross on earth. He was burdened with men's sins, trying to carry out His Father's plan amid ridicule, persecution, and loneliness. He was commissioned by God to save man, and He did it with humility, forgiveness, and love. Though suffering the worst humiliation and rejection by a tortuous death, His self-sacrifice on the cross was the epitome of love and grace.

I was beginning to see more clearly that no matter where my family stood in their individual relationships with Christ, if I was a true disciple of the living Lord, I would need to carry my personal burdens, too. Christ carried His cross while making the ultimate sacrifice for us. What

My Spiritual Sacrifices

was my sacrifice? What could I give up or surrender to God that would be pleasing to Him? Didn't I already know the answer? Hadn't God reminded me over and over what He wanted from me? Yes, I knew. He wanted me to sacrifice my feelings of discouragement and alienation, and instead focus on Him. He wanted my thankful heart and my rejoicing spirit, even in the midst of heartache, disappointment, and difficulty. Hadn't Christ done so much for me? Living each day, no matter what the challenges or circumstances, I needed to demonstrate my love for God with my spiritual sacrifices of gratitude, praise, and worship.

Lord, help me cling to You as my example. Don't let me fall into the futile trap of self-pity. Help me to have Your fortitude, Your thankful heart, and Your overflowing joy even in the midst of strife. I know I can succeed only with the help of Your divine Holy Spirit. You are so awesome, and I love You so much.

> *Jesus said, "For whoever does the will of God, he is My brother and sister and mother."* Mark 3:35 (NASB)

April 2002

31

WHAT DOES EASTER MEAN?

The following is a letter I wrote to Kevin's Cambodian girlfriend of almost three years, after she asked me what Easter means to Christians.

April 16, 2002

Dear Mo,

I wanted to share with you a little more about what Easter means to Christians in general, and to me personally. It was difficult to elaborate in the kitchen on Easter Sunday when you first asked me.

Christians believe that we are separated from God by sin (that's anything that gets in the way of our having a perfect relationship with our holy and righteous God). Sin began way back with the first two people on earth, Adam and Eve, when they disobeyed God and put their own desires before Him. Even though people don't like to think of themselves as sinners, we all fall short of God's perfect standard. The Bible says in Romans 3:23, "... *for all have sinned and fall short of the glory of God.*" God wants a perfect and fulfilling relationship with us, but our sin (selfishness, rejection of Him, self-focus, pride, own agenda) gets in the way.

What Does Easter Mean?

God's plan was, and always has been, to send His Son, the exact likeness of Himself (God incarnate) to earth to be a human. People would come to know Him and love Him, and through His Word (the Bible), future generations would come to know Him too. God's plan always has been to break the power of sin, death, and separation from Him through the sacrifice of His Son on the cross.

What exactly does that mean? No matter how hard we work at it, on our own we can't remove sin. That's why God sent His Son, Jesus Christ, to save sinners. With that one sacrificial act of God whereby His Son took all of our sins upon Himself and died in our place, we are spared from an eternity separated from God. When Christ rose three days after He had been crucified and ascended into heaven, it clearly demonstrated that Satan no longer had the power of death over Him or over us.

What is our part in all of this? God just wants us to simply believe that Christ did that for us and trust Christ as our merciful Savior. One of the most quoted verses in the Bible, John 3:16, tells us about that loving act: *"For God so loved the world that he gave His only begotten Son, that whoever believes in Him shall not perish, but have eternal life."*

I know this might all sound unbelievable, but God's ways are not man's ways. God wants us to rely on Him, not ourselves. He gives salvation as a gift, not as a reward for our efforts, because the standard would always be unattainable for us. This way, too, everyone anywhere may receive salvation, no matter who he or she is, by simply believing in Christ. This humble trust would glorify and elevate God, not ourselves. When we believe that faith in Jesus Christ to remove our sin is the only way to God, it's very humbling.

There's something else God does for us that is equally amazing. He fills that selfish, sinful void, which formerly took up so much of our inner selves, with His Holy

Spirit. So now God lives within us, changing our lives dramatically. We act and think differently because part of God actually lives within us. Our greatest desire becomes wanting to know Him more, spending time with Him, reading His Word, praying, and worshipping Him.

I know this is all true because I finally surrendered my will to God after resisting for many years, and I asked God to take all that I wasn't and put it into everything He is. I knew in my heart that I was unworthy, and I finally recognized the fact that I would never be acceptable to our holy God without Christ's help to remove my sin. I would never be able to do enough good works to work my way to God. I desperately needed a Savior, and I wanted to be certain where I was going after I died.

That was sixteen years ago, and my life has not been the same since. I know that God loves me and that He will never leave me or forsake me here on earth, or ever. I trust Him, and I trust His Word, the Bible. This personal relationship with a living God has brought much fulfillment and peace to my life.

After studying different religions, it is interesting to note that Christianity is the only religion in which we seek God not on human terms, but on His terms. We are saved because of what His Son, Jesus Christ, did for us, not on anything we do to make ourselves acceptable. We have heaven to look forward to because of a loving act of our merciful God—fortunately not something based on our untrustworthy merit. Once we are resting in God's work and are filled with His Spirit, we want to grow to be more like Him and love like He does. Any good works we do are a result of His power in us; we do not do these works because we have to try to prove our goodness or worthiness. His power and love make us worthy, which always makes us mindful of our dependence on Him (which is just what He wants!).

What Does Easter Mean?

I hope you don't mind me sharing all this with you, Mo, but I thought you might be interested in knowing more about Christianity since it is our family's faith. Katie received this New Testament on Easter Sunday at our church, and since we have quite a few Bibles already, I wanted to give it to you. It is the essence of the Christian faith. It might be a good idea to start with Matthew, Mark, Luke, or John so that you learn about the life of Jesus. These four books were written firsthand by four of His disciples who spent a lot of time with Him. I hope this will be helpful. Let me know if you have any more questions. I'm always here.

Lovingly,
Barbara

32

WE DON'T NEED A U-HAUL

I once heard someone remark, "I've never seen a hearse carrying a U-Haul!" That thought struck me as I was slowly snaking my way behind a long line of cars heading for the cemetery that hot August day. The suddenness of this particular death had come as a shock to everyone. Kitty, the deceased, was the forty-seven-year-old mother of one of my daughter's best friends. One evening last week she was experiencing an excruciating headache, along with feeling extremely nauseated. Because the onset was so immediate and severe, her neighbor called the paramedics. By the time the ambulance arrived at the hospital, which was only seven minutes from her home, Kitty was in a coma. After three days in intensive care, she was still in a coma. Tests indicated she had experienced a fatal brain aneurysm. "One of the worst," a nurse declared.

How could this be? My daughter, Katie, had just been vacationing with Kitty and her daughter, Laura, two weeks before, and all was well. They had had a terrific time and were already planning their next trip. Everyone who knew Kitty was stunned. Everyone was keenly aware, too, that this left Laura with no immediate family, just a couple distant relatives.

At times like this, all the stresses, frustrations, and problems of daily living become very miniscule. Those all-consuming preoccupations of life become insignificant and inconsequential when we recognize our lives could end in an instant. Staring us in the face at times like this is the bigger all-important question: What happens to us after we die?

Our spiritual walk is often put aside in our busyness. We figure we'll deal with those spiritual issues when we have more time, or when we're older, maybe closer to the end of our lives. We write wills and living trusts to determine what will happen to all our material accumulations. We purchase plots where we will be buried, and sometimes we even decide what will be said at our funeral.

Shouldn't we be even a little concerned about what will happen to our souls? Jesus rightly stated that we are so caught up in all the details of life and that *"there is really only one thing worth being concerned about."*[1] Don't we need the peaceful assurance that when our time comes, whether that be tomorrow or years from now, God will embrace us into His loving arms for all eternity because He knows us personally?

We need to get to know God, spend time reading His Word, and find out what He desires for each of our lives. We need to give some of our valuable and precious time to growing spiritually. As Christ said, *"Yes, every man is a fool who gets rich on earth, but not in heaven."*[2] At times like this, we cannot refute the Bible's declaration that *"the world and its desires pass away,"*[3] but can we also embrace as truth the continuation of that verse: *"... but whoever does the will of God lives forever."*[4] The Bible reiterates this truth over and over again: *"... if anyone keeps My Word, he will never see death."*[5] We would be at peace, not only throughout our lives but also when our time comes, if we were to know this and believe it. It seems that our friends and family would also feel that same blessed assurance when it came time to say good-bye to our earthly bodies, knowing that we would be *"absent from the body"* but *"home with the Lord."*[6]

One thing is for sure—none of us will need a U-haul.

What I Want
(Psalms 27:4, 104:33–34)

What I want from God, what I seek, not wanting more,
is to praise and worship Him, my precious, holy Lord,
to live in His presence and to lift up His name,
delighting in His perfect peace and promised future gain.

God in My Life

I will always sing to Him 'til every breath is gone,
then my glorious praise in heaven will continue on.
May the Lord be pleased with everything I have to give.
He's the source of all my joy; in Him I'll always live.

August 2002

33

LOVE THAT KNOWS NO BOUNDS

It was Sunday, November 10, and George and I had driven about a half an hour from our house to pick up my mother for her eighty-second birthday. We had planned to return home for a family dinner and have her stay overnight. The roast was in the oven, the potatoes were ready to go in, and the low-calorie birthday dessert was in the refrigerator (both Mom and my youngest daughter, Katie, were on Weight Watchers). My older daughter, Kim, had come home from college, about two hours away, to join the celebration. I had left instructions for both girls to set and decorate the table and watch over the cooking of the dinner while we were gone.

George and I arrived at Mom's door but were surprised to see her sitting on the couch and mumbling, "I don't feel well. I have felt sick all night."

"That's awful," I responded, "and it's your birthday!" She was even having difficulty talking.

We felt this was serious enough that we should take her to an urgent care facility. We almost parked inside to get as close as we could to the front door, but even so, it was a slow and arduous walk to the reception area for Mom.

In between moans, she kept repeating, "I just don't feel well."

That wasn't like Mom, who complains very little and has a very high tolerance to pain.

After filling out all the paperwork, the receptionist commented that there was a two-hour wait.

Oh no, I thought, *we can't wait that long!*

We decided to take Mom to a walk-in medical center close to our house, even though it would take thirty minutes to get there. Once underway, that was the *longest* thirty minutes imaginable! Mom's eyes were closed the entire trip, and with her head down, she occasionally let out a low, painful groan.

Once again, we got as close to the front door as possible and managed to get Mom inside, almost lifting her along the way. As soon as we stopped in the waiting area, I was concerned. There were many more people waiting to be seen than usual.

Oh no, I thought once again.

I explained Mom's dire situation to the receptionist, but she said that unfortunately there was about a two-hour wait, or possibly more. I could feel the panic rising as I tried my best to remain calm. I continued pleading for Mom to be seen sooner as I watched her with her head down, obviously in a great deal of pain.

"It's her eighty-second birthday today!" I found myself announcing to the receptionist. Seeing our concern, she allowed us to wait in a separate small room inside, but she indicated that there was only one doctor on staff at the moment.

A nurse assistant came in and took Mom's temperature: normal. She took Mom's blood pressure: normal. Mom was not sick to her stomach. It was all very baffling, but she continued to complain, saying, "I just don't feel well."

I said, once again, to the nurse this time, "And can you believe it's her birthday!"

About twenty minutes later, a doctor appeared. *Thank goodness*, I thought, feeling immediate relief.

The doctor asked Mom several questions and then performed a quick examination. I said to him, "Can you believe it's her birthday today?"

Mom more specifically complained of pain in the abdominal area, and after pressing that area, the doctor concluded, "I think you should go to the hospital for a CAT scan."

To our surprise, Mom stated with emphatic clarity, "I'm *not* going to the hospital!"

George didn't hesitate to respond. "We're *going* to the hospital!"

We thanked the doctor and once again headed back toward Mom's house, since the hospital where her insurance was accepted was there. We called the kids and told them to go ahead and eat the birthday dinner, as we didn't know when we would be back.

It seemed like forever again as we drove back, but we finally reached the emergency room of the hospital. To our relief, they took Mom right away. After a barrage of questions, the doctor said it would take about four hours to prepare her for the CAT scan and proceed with it, so he suggested we leave, go eat dinner, and come back in a few hours.

Since Kim had made a special effort to drive home from college to be with the family, we drove back home to see her for a few minutes and have some left-over birthday dinner. George stayed home while I drove back to the hospital again, arriving at about 8:00 p.m. I arrived just in time to wave to Mom as she was wheeled away to have her CAT scan.

After returning from that procedure, it surprised me that Mom was hooked up to an IV. When I asked why, the nurse responded, "We're giving her antibiotics." A heart monitor beeped behind her, resonating loudly throughout the entire emergency area. Whenever I posed a question to the nurses or attendants, their responses were vague and unsure. What was going on?

At about 10:00 p.m., a doctor appeared who stated, "She will need surgery."

I inquired, "When? In a couple days? A week?"

His firm answer was "Now! We're prepping her for surgery." The emergency surgery team was being assembled at that very moment.

Once again I sputtered, "But it's her birthday!"

At that point, it didn't seem to matter. Apparently, the doctors had detected "free air" escaping from her bowels, which could put toxins into her system. This could potentially be extremely serious. There was no decision to be made and no second opinions. The surgery would be taking place in two hours. I was stunned! Mom had not complained of intestinal problems prior to that day. She had been relatively healthy.

At midnight at the end of Mom's eighty-second birthday, emergency surgery began. My brother, Curt, and sister-in-law, Eileen, joined me in the waiting area as we talked, prayed, and waited anxiously. The doctor appeared to report that most of the surgery had been spent trying to find the hole. At that juncture, the hole, a perforated ulcer, was very small. Mom was stitched back together with a long and painful recovery ahead: two days in ICU, several days in DOU, a week altogether in the hospital, and at least a week in a nursing care facility, plus more recovery at home.

The next day, I was in and out of the hospital checking on Mom. Her incision was painful, especially when she coughed. She was getting nauseated from the morphine they were administering through her IV. I felt so badly for Mom as I drove home that night. Everything had been so sudden, extreme, and unexpected. Was the surgery necessary? Had the right decision been made? Somehow, I felt responsible.

It was 4:00 a.m. the next morning when I awoke with a start. There was a sharp pain centered in my chest near my heart, but slightly running downward. I sat upright, pressing my chest. Breathing deeply was difficult because of the pain. I sat up in bed for a while, trying to figure out what was happening. I hadn't ever felt this kind of pain before, and it wasn't going away. George had awakened, and he suggested, "Why don't you try taking an aspirin."

After swallowing two pills, I was hoping the pain would subside. I felt a little better, but even when the alarm went off at 5:20 a.m., I still had a residual dull pain in my chest.

That entire day I did not feel well, and to my dismay, I also had the hiccups on and off about five times. I rarely get the hiccups. I couldn't even remember the last time I had had the hiccups, it happened so infrequently. These hiccups came instantly and left just as quickly. *This is so strange*, I thought.

All of a sudden it occurred to me that I had seen Mom get the hiccups several times in the hospital as her body was trying to reorient after the surgery. It also dawned on me that the pain in my chest may have been my subconscious attempt to transfer her pain to myself. I dismissed the idea. Why would I have pain running down my chest when Mom had had her surgery in the intestinal area?

A few days later, when I visited Mom in the hospital, I offhandedly asked her where her incision was from the surgery. She showed me her bandages covering her multiple stitches. There it was, running down her chest, from near her heart to her belly button. I almost gasped! That was right where my pain had been centered. In my mind I thought her procedure had taken place in the intestinal area, but in my heart, unknowingly, I must have sensed where it had actually occurred. Could I have really been trying to transfer her pain to myself? Could I have made myself have the hiccups?

I looked up the word "hiccups" in the dictionary, and the definition began, "a sudden involuntary contraction of the diaphragm ..." The word "involuntary" immediately caught my attention. There's no way I could have *made* myself have hiccups. I wondered again, "Can a person really transfer pain from someone else on to oneself?" I didn't know anyone who had ever done that.

After more pondering, however, I suddenly realized I *did* know someone who had done that. In fact, I knew someone who had done that not only for me but for many others as well. Hadn't Jesus Christ taken the pain, the burdens, the sins of everyone upon Himself to spare everyone from going through the same pain of dying and being separated from God for all eternity? Didn't Christ suffer the grief we should have rightfully endured? The Bible says, *"He himself bore our sins in his body on the cross, so that we might die to sins and live to righteousness."*[1] This was not just a figurative interpretation of Christ's sacrifice. Christ literally took our sins and bore our pain so we would not have to experience it. He loved us so much that He was willing to die in our place and suffer anguish beyond our comprehension so that we would be made right with a holy, righteous God.

I can't help but feel that Christ looks down upon us and weeps when we are in pain or going through difficult times. He wants us to cast our burdens upon Him, for He will bear the pain and bring us His peace. In His omnipotence and love, He can do that for us. We must put our faith in His ability and believe in Him.

Thank you, Lord, for making me cognizant of Your indescribable grace and mercy. Thank you for giving me insight into Your miraculous act of compassion. Your love is real. It continues to reach down and personally touch our lives every day, knowing no bounds.

November 2002

34

A Christmas to Remember

Because it was December, I started reminiscing about my childhood Christmases when I lived with my mom, dad, older sister, and younger brother. It was easy to remember the year I received my baby doll, Susie, and another year when my present was the more grown-up doll, Margie, with her accompanying wardrobe, purchased from our church bazaar. All of us kids went on a scavenger hunt another Christmas to find our fishing poles and gear. I remember the exact sweaters my sister, Nancy, and I received one Christmas when we were teens; it was the same year we got our guitar.

One particular Christmas, however, stands out more than the rest. It wasn't because of something *I* received, but a gift my mother was given from my father. It was not an unusual or expensive gift, but it was the story that went with it that made it so meaningful and memorable. This story goes back to the 1920s, when my mother was a little girl.

When my mother and her brother were young, they each had small bank accounts. Their aunts and uncles, who could afford it, always remembered them on birthdays and at Christmastime by giving them some change (or sometimes even a whole dollar) to put into their accounts. Their parents would add to these accounts when possible. My mom and her brother were saving up every penny to reach their goal of purchasing their very own two-wheel bikes.

My mom's family, along with many others, endured some difficult years during the 1930s because of the Depression. My mom's dad was a builder and carpenter, but there was no work. They had been living in a beautiful home in New Jersey, but because their family was desperate for money, they sold it for a mere seven thousand dollars. As my mother added, "Our family practically gave it away!"

They had to move to their summer home in Twin Lakes, Pennsylvania. There was no electricity and no running water. They planted a garden, and their neighbor gave them milk from his cow. Meat was expensive to buy, so my mother's father killed deer, which they turned into roasts, hamburger, soup, and whatever they could create.

My mom explained that at the time they moved to Twin Lakes, both she and her brother had about twenty-five dollars in their accounts, which would have been just about the right amount to purchase the bikes. Even though her father found a few odd jobs to do, the family was still suffering financially. Her mother was unable to work as a teacher because once a woman got married, at that time, she did not continue to work in the teaching profession.

Their family became destitute. Not wanting to go on welfare, my mom's dad took the bike money out of both accounts to buy groceries for the family. In later years, that money was never replaced. In fact, it was never spoken about again. So my mom never received her long-awaited bike; that is, until that special Christmas when we all got to watch her, at the age of forty-three, unveil her present—a brand-new shiny two-wheel bike!

As tears filled her eyes and started streaming down her face, it did not take long for all of us to join in, crying right along with her. We all knew what this special gift meant to her, and we were all filled with mixed emotions of sorrow for what she had grown up without, and joy that it was finally fulfilled that day. As my mother unsteadily, but happily, rode her lovely new bike down our street, I couldn't help but realize how lucky I was. We were not the richest family, by far, but we were never lacking for what we needed.

And now that I'm older and writing this memory, I know I have been blessed in ways too numerous to count. I am so thankful for all that God has given me. I am rich indeed, not only because I have been blessed with a beautiful family and wonderful friends, but most of all because I have a relationship with an almighty God who loves me and will always provide for me.

A Christmas to Remember

Heavenly Father, I hope I will always be mindful of what I have, and praise You for all the blessings in my life. I am so thankful.

Because the Lord is my Shepherd, I have everything I need ... (Psalm 23:1 LB)

December 2002

35

God's Wisdom Can Make a Change

Lately, I had been perturbed that a fellow member of an organization I belonged to always looked at everyone else as the problem rather than looking at herself. She held her opinion (on everything) in the utmost regard, didn't attentively consider others' points of view, was ready to come to her own defense in all discussions, and was often argumentative. She just would not back down. I found myself arguing back, which I normally try not to do, because I was trying to get her to see what she was doing—arguing for the sake of arguing.

In fact, this woman had just broken her engagement to her fiancé because, as she said, "We argue all the time!" She added, "He always thinks he's right!" (Interesting that she could see this flaw in someone else's character but did not have the eyes to see it in herself!) This quarrelsome attitude was making it very unpleasant to participate in something I thought very worthwhile and enjoyed otherwise. I didn't want to give it up. Didn't she see that she was making the whole atmosphere very uncomfortable for everyone? I started praying that this woman would be less defensive, less prideful, and more open to a changed heart.

It didn't surprise me that today and yesterday in my Bible study of James, we took a close look at the difference between Godly wisdom and earthly wisdom. Earthly wisdom is described as *"earthy, natural, and demonic where jealousy and selfish ambition exist"* and *"there is disorder and every evil thing."*[1] God gets right down to business when He states that a person with only earthly wisdom is a "fool."[2] According to the wise book of Proverbs, here are some characteristics of a fool (NASB):

- 1:7—despises wisdom and instruction
- 14:16—is arrogant and haughty
- 15:5—rejects his father's instruction
- 18:2—desires only to give opinions
- 18:6—his mouth brings strife
- 20:3—will be quarrelsome
- 29:11—loses his temper

And, of course, "his" could easily be changed to "her."

What great insight into the things pride and arrogance bring to one's life! I knew this because I was experiencing the contentious and abrasive result. I, for one, did not want to be considered a fool by God.

The following Scriptures capture the difference between earthly wisdom and godly wisdom, and the results of both in our lives. Here are characteristics of a person with godly wisdom (NASB):

- Proverbs 10:12—responds to all transgressions with love
- Proverbs 13:10—is willing to receive counsel
- Proverbs 20:3—keeps away from strife
- 2 Timothy 2:24—is kind to all and able to teach; is patient when wronged.
- 2 Timothy 2:14—does not wrangle with words, as it leads to the ruin of the hearer

The Bible explains that if we seek God's wisdom and are obedient to His commands, we will have wisdom from above that is *"first pure, then peaceable, gentle, reasonable, full of mercy and good fruits ..."*[3] We will be marked as different from the world because we strive for peace at all times. That means we focus on God and His goodness, not just thinking of ourselves and "having to be right" all the time. God wants us to be able to admit our weaknesses, accept correction, and "*live at peace with everyone*,"[4] responding with unconditional love. We should remain calm and self-controlled, not be easily provoked, and show compassion. That, we all know, is a huge task!

We need to be reminded every day that God showed us mercy and forgiveness when He sent His Son, Jesus Christ, to die on a cross in our place. Likewise, we should show that same unselfish love and kindness to others. God says that if we can get our self out of the way and make loving God and others our main focus (with the help of His Holy Spirit), we will receive the blessings of the fruit of the Spirit: love, joy, peace, patience, kindness, goodness, faithfulness, gentleness, and self-control.[5]

Lord, Your Word continues to amaze me with its perfect and specific lessons for our lives. Your Spirit is actively working and alive, teaching and correcting us so that love can reign supreme in our relationships with others. What a changed world we would have if we all heeded Your instructions! Help me, Lord, to obey.

October 2003

36

A Mother's Prayer

After reading Isaiah 42, which is about how the Israelites had sinned against God, it was a relief to read in Isaiah 43:1–7 that the time of exile in Babylon was almost over and God was ready to bring His people back to safety and security. I read with interest God's reassuring words to the Israelites: "I will bring your offspring from the east, and gather you from the west. I will say to the north, 'Give them up!' And to the south, 'Do not hold them back.' Bring my sons from afar and my daughters from the ends of the earth."[1]

Instantly, I thought of my own children, now in their teens and twenties. Hadn't I so often interceded through prayer on their behalf, pleading with God to draw them back to His presence when they wandered away, asking Him to protect them and hold them close? I heard myself inwardly crying out again, Oh Lord, in Your omnipotent power and merciful love, call forth my children being held captive in this world. Gather them from wherever they are—at school, at work, at home, or with friends. Do not allow anything to hold them up, block their path, or dull their hearing. Help them clearly hear You calling them by name. I know you would be saying…

"Come to Me, Kim, Kevin, and Katie. You are precious in My sight.[2] I love you far greater than any earthly parent could. I created you for My glory.[3] Know that I am continually with you[4] from the time you wake up in the morning until you rest your head at night. While you are sleeping, I watch over you. When you wade through rivers overflowing with life's difficulties, when you walk through sinking sands of self-doubt, or feel consumed by dark clouds of uncertainty, do not be afraid. I am right by your side, and I will never fail you.[5] I make a way for you to surface from deep seas of discouragement, and offer a straight roadway when you are lost and wandering in empty wilderness. Do you understand low long, how wide, how deep, and how high my love really is for you?[6] I love you so much that I have made sure nothing keeps you from me. I have sent My Son from heaven to earth, to die for you, because I am not willing to live without you. I created each of you differently, with your own distinct personality and temperament. I also created each of you in My image[7] to be a reflection of My grace, mercy, and love. You are My children. I made you so I could love you, and I just want you to love Me back. I long for your companionship. I am never far away."

Right after writing the above, I picked up the book I was reading—*Leota's Garden*, by Francine Rivers. The first words I read were those of the main character, eighty-four-year-old Leota, who was estranged from her two grown children and voicing her despair to her loving Father: "Oh, Lord God, I ache for my children. I love them so much … my lambs are lost. Will they even recognize Your voice when You call to them? Will they cry out in relief and run to You? Or will they turn a deaf ear? Will they hear, but run away from the hand that reaches out to rescue them?"[8]

I wondered how many other mothers of the world were on their knees, humbling themselves before God for their children's sake. I knew I was not alone. In fact, a book I had recently read, *When Mothers Pray*, gave several examples of devoted Christian mothers in history who had diligently prayed for their lost sons or daughters.

One of these stories was about the mother of Augustine, whose wayward son eventually became a notable leader of the Church. Growing up, her son lived with a mistress at the age of sixteen, fathered an illegitimate son, and joined a cult. His mother prayed for him for over nineteen years. Augustine described the impact of those prayers after his conversion: "And now didst thou stretch forth thy hand from above and didst draw my soul up and out of that profound darkness because my mother, thy faithful one, wept to Thee on my behalf more than mothers are accustomed to weep for the bodily deaths of their children."[9]

Some early memories of John Newton, preacher and hymn writer, were of his godly mother, who "devoted herself to nurturing his soul," despite her poor health. Though she died early in his life, when he was around seven, he later recalled "her many tears for him." He went on to write such great hymns as "All Troubles Assail Us" and "Amazing Grace," and he credits his mother, saying, "It's hard to shake off a mother's influence."[10]

In his testimony, Scottish doctor W. P. MacKay, author of the hymn "Revive Us Again," said his godly mother often talked to him about the Savior. He stated, "Many times I witnessed her wrestling in prayer for my soul's salvation." Nothing, however, made a deep impression on him, and he admitted, "the older I grew, the more wicked I became."[11] The turning point came later in his life, when a patient under his care died with very few possessions except for a Bible that he coveted and read religiously. When William MacKay examined the Bible closely, he could not believe what he saw. It was a Bible *his* mother had given him, with his name still in it in his mother's hand, which he had sold for a small amount of money. MacKay said that this event was the cause of his conversion.

Often, it seems that those who eventually become great ministers or evangelists were at one time the most rebellious and furthest from God in their youth. Their mothers prayed earnestly because they knew it was a spiritual battle for their children's souls. From these testimonies and others, it is encouraging to witness God's convicting power that turned these lives around, especially when it is an answer to their mothers' desperate prayers.

Being diligent in prayer is not easy, especially when years pass and progress is slow. However, dwelling on what is not happening robs one of joy in the Lord. It also gives smug satisfaction to the Enemy.

When I worry, it shows my lack of faith in God's ability and power. I can choose to worry, or I can worship. I want to be obedient to apostle Paul's words as he encouraged fellow Christians: *"rejoice always, pray without ceasing, and give thanks in all circumstances for this is the will of God in Jesus Christ."*[12]

I know I must continue to claim my children for Jesus and pray for them with every ounce of my being. I must focus on what *can* happen and what God *will* do in His timing, not on what isn't happening. As Ruth Bell Graham stated in *Prodigals and Those Who Love Them*, "As a mother, I must faithfully, patiently, lovingly, and happily do my part – then quietly wait for God to do His."[13] It is through reminders like these that I am assured that my prayers are never lost, but are in God's keeping until He gives me an answer.

As I continued to read my book that night, I could see that even Leota began to realize the futility of negative thinking when she concluded, "Maybe there is hope yet … Oh, Lord, I will hold tight to my love and not let go … I will cast away anger and hurt and despair. I will think about You."[14]

Lord, I want to be like Leota. I want to think about all that is possible in You. Help me to focus on what is right and true and good, and all that you have planned for my children. They are Your *"workmanship created in Christ Jesus for good works,"* which I know you have prepared in advance for them.[15] I will hold on to that promise, and I will pray.

July 2005

37

WHO NEEDS TO CHANGE?

Lately, I have been perplexed by a friend, Sandy, who is such a vivacious, enthusiastic Christian, taking mission trips to foreign countries and always trying to do good in the community, but who does not always show a Christian attitude in other ways. She continually wants to take charge and take over no matter what, not delegating; and she actually seems quite thoughtless sometimes, putting herself and her needs first. It's been bothering me that a fellow Christian who appears to be so good and caring doesn't see her lack of courtesy in her day-to-day interactions with others.

When doing my Bible study today, it asked us to list what we thought would be good instructions for individual members of the Christian body to follow in dealing with fellow believers, and my immediate thoughts were that individuals need to

- be focused on others,
- lift others up,
- care about the needs of others, and
- put others before self.

That looked like the perfect list in my mind (and of course, I was thinking of Sandy).

We were directed to read Colossians 3:12–14: "*So, as those who have been chosen of God, holy and beloved, put on a heart of compassion, kindness, humility, gentleness, and patience, bearing with one another and forgiving each other, whoever has a complaint against anyone, just as the Lord forgave you, so also should you. Beyond all these things, put on love, which is the perfect bond of unity."*[1]

Wow! I immediately knew that God was speaking to me through this Scripture. I really felt that God was convicting me that the heart of the problem was not with the *other* person, but rather with how I perceived that person; that the focus should be on *my* heart and *my* attitude. I needed to acquire the eyes, ears, and heart of God Himself, who doesn't react to situations or deal with people based on momentary feelings or pride, but makes love a choice—one with unconditional loving-kindness. It was obvious that my demeanor (and attitude) was showing nothing of the compassionate and forgiving presence of God within, but just resentment, bitterness, and ill will, which was giving the Prince of Darkness the upper hand in my life. Didn't apostle Paul even caution the Philippians about *"grumbling or disputing"*[2] among each other, knowing that these would be major hindrances to building God's kingdom, and major contributors to crushing joy?

God forgave us and gave us His Holy Spirit, a part of Himself, so we could act differently and respond differently than the world around us. I needed to allow God's love to overshadow my inadequate and ineffective way of dealing with a fellow Christian—and everyone else, for that matter. After all, if He had based His salvation on my worthiness, I never would have been acceptable in His sight. Thank goodness God does not deal in the realm of rationale and reason, or He would never have saved me. The Bible reassures us that *"God, being rich in mercy, because of His great love with which He loved us, even when we were dead in our transgressions, made us alive together with Christ ... by grace (we) have been saved through faith."*[3]

It was obvious that I needed a readjusted focus. It was not my friend who needed to change; it was me. That's what would make a difference for Christ—for me to respond not like the world, but to mirror Christ's image. That's what would make an impact in building God's kingdom.

Lord, You are so amazing and so good. You see into my heart and know what I need. Thank you for causing the Bible to speak to me so personally with just the right words at the right time. Lead me in the right direction to be different in my responses. I know I need to be less critical and more forgiving. Keep me focused on needed changes within myself. It's Your purpose and Your plans that I desire. I want others to see You in me. May I be a worthy witness of Your glory. Amen!

I have a newly-made magnet on my refrigerator. It says, "I only see the good in you!"

April 2006

38

A God of Love

It was the last week of July, and our family, including all the extended family of aunts, uncles, and cousins, was getting ready for our vacation together in Hawaii to celebrate my mom's eighty-fifth birthday. We had wanted to do something special for this grand occasion, and since my brother's family had already made arrangements to use their time-share in Maui starting August 5, we rented an additional condo nearby so we could all be together. We had been looking forward to this vacation since November, Mom's actual birthday month, and at last were packing and making more detailed plans.

In the midst of the packing, my sister-in-law called with startling and unexpected news. My brother, Curt, had been short of breath and feeling extremely tired, so they had gone to the doctors to see what was amiss. Knowing there are heart problems in our family, the heart is always on our minds. Thankfully, Curt's heart was fine. What she had to say next, however, stunned us all! Curt's blood was indicating possible leukemia, and a few days later, further tests confirmed it. We were all in shock!

We all wondered how Curt could have leukemia. After researching the disease, I know that it is not genetic, even though my grandfather apparently had a form of it. It is also not environmental, even though Curt's business involved working with chemicals. The doctors indicated that none of these were contributing factors. Leukemia is caused after birth by a change in the DNA, and the type that Curt had, AML (acute mylogenous leukemia), was an aggressive, fast-replicating type.

In disbelief, we soon learned that only by chemo treatment would Curt have a chance to survive this serious illness. Without it, he might have only a few months to live. Oh, Lord! How could this be? How could my otherwise healthy brother have such a sudden life-threatening disease? I found myself repeating over and over, "Help him, Lord. In Your mercy, and by Your healing hand!"

Time just stood still. We didn't know whether to continue packing for Hawaii or not. After all, we were planning to stay in my brother's timeshare. How could we go without both my brother and my sister-in-law? After several phone calls back and forth, my brother convinced us we should all go anyway and they would look into getting a refund for their scheduled flights. We all knew it was going to be a different vacation.

I saw Curt two days before I left for Hawaii. I drove to the hospital, where he was already hooked up to an IV, receiving the twenty-four-hour chemo. This would go on for a week. At that point, he was not in too much pain except for the area in his hip where they had drawn bone marrow. On that Thursday, the Red Cross just happened to be there for a blood drive, so my sister-in-law and I went downstairs to donate. It was amazing to me how many of the hospital employees were donating blood, a number of them donating in Curt's name. Eileen and I had lunch together, and even in the gravity of this situation, I remember saying to her, "I can't help but feel that there is a purpose behind all of this."

We left for Hawaii with Curt on our minds. While we were there, we made sure we took time to pray together for him, and someone called him daily. I said silent prayers whenever I thought of him.

When we got back home, Curt had finished his first round of week-long chemo. It was obvious that the chemo was having an effect. His leukemia count had gone from 90 percent to 35 percent. Unfortunately, it was also having a critically negative impact on the rest of his body. His kidneys were failing, his temperature zoomed up to 103.6 degrees, his blood pressure dropped to a low of 83 over 35, his blood sugar level was out of control, skyrocketing up to 500 (normal is 90–110). He was given strong antibiotics and insulin.

Curt was fighting for his life. We saw him several times during this short period of time. We took Mom to see him the day he was put on dialysis, the same day we headed to Las Vegas for his son's wedding. (Could it have been any worse?). He was not totally cognizant of everything going on and said very little. It was hard for him to concentrate because of the toxins in his kidneys. It was very scary.

All of our family had sent out the word about Curt, asking for prayer on his behalf. He was in such a critical condition and had been in ICU now for several weeks. All of us were still in a state of shock, wondering how this could be happening. It just didn't seem fair. *Lord, Curt needs you*, I thought. *Help him to see his need of You.*

Some of us in the family were also praying that this would be the turning point for Curt in accepting Jesus Christ as his Lord and Savior. There were others joining in with the same prayer request. None of us knew what the future held, and we were worried about Curt's soul. He needed that peace and assurance that he was safe in God's hands, but what we saw when we looked into his eyes was fear.

Oh, Curt, I pray that you would know Christ personally, and know just how much He loves you and is right by your side. Do you feel Him reaching out to you, beseeching, "Trust Me, I am with you. Accept what I have done—that I have died on the cross for you. I died in *your* place, with *your* sin upon Me, so that when you die, your sin will not keep us apart, and we can be together in heaven forever." Are you listening, Curt? God is just asking you to trust Him and surrender your life to Him.

Before all this happened, I think Curt was so busy with everyday preoccupations that he didn't give God much thought. However, when you have nothing else to do but lie on a hospital bed, staring at the walls with time passing slowly, there is a lot of time for introspection. Questions come to mind, such as, "What is the purpose of life? Have I done all that I was meant to do? Am I certain of where I am going after I die?"

I'm sure Curt had lots of time to evaluate his life and think about the future. How would he react? Would he be bitter, maybe even angry with God? I once heard it said, "You'll never know that God is all you need until God is all you've got." Would Curt see his desperate need to get right with God and cry out in desperation for Jesus to save him? Would he acknowledge his sin that separated him from God, and humbly ask for forgiveness?

A God of Love

I had sent out several e-mails to friends and phoned friends, explaining Curt's critical situation asking them to pray for him. I told everyone I saw of my brother's plight, always requesting intercessory prayer. I called my church, and the pastor prayed with me. Other family members were sending out the word about Curt, asking for prayer. I don't think any of us realized how far-reaching these urgent appeals traveled. There were whole Bible study groups and churches praying for him.

George and I visited Curt in the hospital on Sunday, August 27. Thankfully, he was now out of ICU, his kidneys had stabilized, and his temperature, sugar level, and blood pressure were back in normal ranges. We were all encouraging him to eat, because he needed to get his energy back up for the second round of chemo starting the next day. It would be the same twenty-four-hour nonstop treatment, but this time it would last for five days. I knew he was not looking forward to the ordeal, but according to the latest blood and bone marrow test, 35 percent of his cells still indicated the dreaded leukemia. No time could be wasted. I remember leaving Curt that night so unsettled and sad, with lots of questions myself. Why did my happy-go-lucky brother, who had already been dealt some heavy blows in life, have to go through something like this? He didn't deserve it!

Well, Curt didn't start the second round of chemo that next day as planned. With fortunate news that a bed had opened up at a well-respected cancer facility nearby, he was taken there by ambulance on Tuesday. He was expected to begin his second round of chemo right away. However, after additional blood tests and a bone marrow test were done, the results indicated (are you ready?) no leukemia in his body! He was declared to be in complete remission. To have absolutely no leukemia cells in your body after just one round of chemo is truly an answer to prayer. I have never personally known anyone who has had leukemia before Curt, but I had heard some leukemia stories from friends, and no one had said anyone went into complete remission after just one chemo treatment.

I knew that Curt still had things to face ahead—possibly more chemo and a bone marrow transplant—but at the moment, all I could do was thank God for being so good to Curt. After what had been going on just two short weeks before, the sudden turnaround was incredible! Curt said that even the doctors seemed baffled at the sudden change in the blood and bone marrow tests.

Time will only tell what's up ahead. All I know right now is that God loves Curt as He does all of us. He was there with him every moment he was in the hospital and felt every pain along with him. God's Son, Jesus Christ, continues to desire a personal relationship with Curt most of all. God is all-powerful and all-knowing and has a better vision of what's best for us than we do.

My Bible study presented me with a timely framed saying at the last meeting. All it says is **"Trust Him."** How true that is. I have to admit there were times during this last month when I began questioning why all this was happening. Now I see clearly, and there's no doubt. God is in control, and we must trust Him in all circumstances, leaving the outcome in His hands.

September 2006

39

Do Not Be Afraid

"I'm afraid!" How many times have we felt this way or even said it out loud?

My brother, Curt, has spoken these words several times in the last couple months and has probably thought it numerous other times. He just finished his second round of chemo and is awaiting results; and he faces a bone marrow transplant in the near future. This is a frightening prospect for anyone.

We had been so relieved after the first round of chemo, when the doctors had sent Curt home early saying he was in complete remission. However, after further investigation of his bone marrow, they found errant leukemia cells that they said were fairly aggressive. When doctors give information about any condition, there's always cause for worry, as they relay all possible scenarios to cover their bases. Fear looms large for any patient, especially since there's lots of down time to worry about all the unknowns up ahead.

In reading the Bible lately, I have become more aware of the numerous times God says, "Fear not" or "Do not be afraid." These words are spoken by God through prophets, kings, and His messenger angels. Christ and His apostles constantly comforted those they encountered with these reassuring words.

There must be good reason why these exact commands are so often repeated throughout the Bible, both in the Old and New Testaments. God made us to love us, but we live in a fallen, sinful world. There are lots of times in life when we have good reason to be afraid. God's Word shows us repeatedly, that He wants us to focus on Him, His presence and His love, not on our circumstances. *"Acquaint now thyself with Him and be at peace."*[1]

As soon as fear rears its ugly head, God exhorts us to fix our thoughts on what is good and pure and right, refusing to dwell on all that is unlike Him. We must cling to God and what is possible. Satan loves fear! It causes worry, anxiety, panic, alarm, confusion, and stress, and it is evil in disguise; this applies to anything that takes our eyes off God. God says we should listen to Him and trust in His providence no matter what's happening around us. *"These things I have spoken to you, so that in Me, you may have peace. In this world you have tribulation, but take courage, I have overcome the world."*[2]

There are many Scriptures in the Old and New Testament exhorting us to not be afraid. Following are just a few from the Bible (NASB):

God Speaks Through the Prophets

Exodus 14:13: *"But Moses said to the people, 'Do not fear! Stand by and see the salvation of the Lord which He will accomplish for you today ... the Lord will fight for you.'"*

Psalm 23:4: *"Even though I walk through the valley of the shadow of death, I will fear no evil, for you are with me; your rod and your staff, they comfort me."*

Psalm 27:1: *"The Lord is my light and my salvation: whom shall I fear?*

Psalm chapters speaking peace to our fears: 27, 46, 49, 56, 91

Proverbs 29:25: *"The fear of man brings a snare, but he who trusts in the Lord will be exalted."*

Isaiah 41:13: *"For I am the Lord your God, who upholds your right hand, Who says to you, "Do not fear, I will help you."'*

Isaiah 43:1b: *"Do not fear, for I have redeemed you; I have called you by name; you are Mine!"*

Isaiah 43:5a: *"Do not fear, for I am with you."*

God Speaks Through His Messenger Angels

Matthew 1:20b: *" ... an angel of the Lord appeared to him in a dream, saying, 'Joseph, son of David, do not be afraid to take Mary as your wife ... '"*

Luke 1:30: *"The angel said to her, 'Do not be afraid, Mary; for you have found favor with God.'"*

Luke 2:10: *"But the angel said to them (the shepherds), 'Do not be afraid; for behold, I bring you good news of great joy which will be for all the people.'"*

Matthew 28:5: *"The angel said to the women, 'Do not be afraid; for I know that you are looking for Jesus who has been crucified.'"*

Jesus Speaks

Mark 4:40 (to the apostles): *"And He said to them, 'Why are you afraid? How is it that you have no faith?'"*

Luke 8:50: *"But when Jesus heard this, He answered him, 'Do not be afraid any longer; only believe, and she will be made well.'"*

Luke 12:32: *"Do not be afraid, little flock, for your Father has chosen gladly to give you the kingdom."*

John 14:27: *"Peace I leave with you; My peace I give to you; not as the world gives do I give to you. Do not let your heart be troubled, nor let it be fearful."*

God Speaks Through the Apostles:

Romans 8:15: *"For you have not received a spirit of slavery leading to fear again, but you have received a spirit of adoption as sons by which we cry out, 'Abba! Father!'"*

2 Timothy 1:7: *"For God has not given us a spirit of timidity, but of power and love and discipline."*

Hebrews 13:5b–6a *" ... for He himself has said, 'I will never desert you, nor will I ever forsake you, so that we confidently say, 'The Lord is my helper, I will not be afraid ... '"*

1 John 4:18: *"There is no fear in love; but perfect love casts out fear, because fear involves punishment, and the one who fears is not perfected in love."*

Revelation 1:17–18a: *"When I saw Him, I fell at His feet ... and He placed His right hand on me, saying, 'Do not be afraid; I am the first and the last and the living One; and I was dead, and behold, I am alive forevermore ... '"*

The next day: October 3

The Word of God is alive and active. It's full of living power, *"piercing as far as the division of soul and spirit, of both joints and marrow ..."*[3] God proves that over and over, and today was no exception. This morning when I started my Bible study, the first Scripture verse I read was Hebrews 4:1: *"Therefore, let us fear if, while a promise remains of entering His rest, anyone of you may seem to have come short of it."*[4]

God said, *"I have sworn in my anger that those who don't believe will never get in ..."*[5]

The biggest fear that we *should* have, then, is *not* believing God and *not* entering His rest. What conquers fear? Faith—knowing our future is with the Lord. Fear ends where faith begins. *"Behold, God is my salvation, I will trust and not be afraid; For the Lord God is my strength and song, And He has become my salvation"* (Isaiah 12:2 NASB).

Lord, You love us so much. Help us to feel Your presence. Let us hear Your voice whispering, "I am here ... do not be afraid." Help us to cling to You. May we feel Your comforting arms protecting us. We need You. Bring us Your peace.

October 2006

40

Deep Roots of Faith

Exasperated, I called to my husband, "Hon, it looks like another plant in the backyard died!"

I just couldn't figure out why we were having so much trouble getting our plants to grow. We had just replanted our entire backyard a few months prior. Both George and I had been so carefully hand watering everything. It was our first priority after getting home from work. Sometimes it took up to forty-five minutes to make sure they all got the proper individual attention.

After this latest plant fatality, I decided to take some of the curled yellow leaves to the nursery for diagnosis. Upon evaluating these specimens, the plant expert concluded, "It looks like you're overwatering!" He continued, "You need to water less often, but do deep watering a couple times a week. The roots are not going deep into the soil, and the plants are not taking hold to help the plants grow like they should."

We were stunned! We had been giving our baby greens such tender, loving care (we thought), not realizing that we had been encouraging only surface growth, not what was needed for mature, deep growth and stability. After thirty years of living in the same house, oftentimes wondering why we were always planting and replanting, this insight was such a wonderful revelation. We were ready and willing to implement this new gardening option. George bought a slow-watering hose, and we carefully wound it through all the plants in the backyard planter.

Now, a few months later, we have done our best to follow this new gardening directive, and I must say we are seeing positive results. The plants are fuller and greener. The flowers are blossoming, and all the plants look healthier and happier.

Strange that this simple gardening experience would make me think of my brother in his recent struggle with leukemia. We had all been fervently praying for his recovery, and our family was so relieved when the doctors had given us the news that Curt was in complete remission. We were ecstatic, calling friends, sending e-mails, and praising God for this unbelievable healing. However, it wasn't more than a few weeks later when we received the news that more cancer cells had been detected. Curt would need to go back for more chemo, plus there was an abnormality with his bone marrow, so a transplant would definitely be necessary. We couldn't help but feel mystified and confused. Why had God let us down after all our praying and faith in His ability to heal Curt completely? Our family had believed in this miracle, and now it had been cruelly taken away.

Fringes of doubt were starting to gather. God, why is this happening? We need you, Lord. Where are you? Why aren't you answering our prayers?

Where were our roots of faith? Were they on the surface or deeply embedded? Because everything wasn't going according to our plans, did that mean that God wasn't listening, that He didn't care about Curt? Questioning God's authority and wisdom would certainly show the shallowness of our roots and our lack of trust in God's plan for Curt's life. Without deep roots, our yellow curled-up leaves were showing. How quickly we were starting to question God's faithfulness, getting discouraged, and doubting His closeness and care.

The Old and New Testaments contain numerous examples of stalwart individuals who grumbled, complained, and blamed God for their plights, even turned their backs on God when things didn't go according to their plans. It's obvious that accepting God's wisdom at all times, no matter what the circumstances, is an ongoing struggle for even the most faithful.

I had just finished reading about Jeremiah, a great prophet of God who constantly begged the Israelites to turn from sin back to God.

He cried out, challenging God: "... *You have failed me in my time of need! You have let them (the Israelites) keep right on with all their persecutions! Your help is as uncertain as a seasonal brook – sometimes a flood, sometimes as dry as a bone!*"[1]

And what was God's response to Jeremiah after that outburst? "*Stop this foolishness and talk some sense! Only if you return to trusting me will I let you continue as my spokesman. You are to influence them, not let them influence you!*"[2]

Additional Scripture tells us we must be like Job, who, after losing everything and everyone of importance in his life, was still able to say, "The Lord gave and the Lord has taken away. Blessed be the name of the Lord."[3] Through all the hardship, pain, and grief, "*Job did not sin nor did he blame God.*" [4]

So often in the Bible, the reason for people's rebellion against God is their lack of trust, their impatience, and their thanklessness. We are not any different. God tells us that faith should not be dependent on circumstances, but in our trusting Him. As Jeremiah pointed out, with only shallow surface roots of faith, we are "*like a stunted shrub in the desert, with no hope for the future, living on the salt-encrusted plains in the barren wilderness ...*" [5] but those who trust God and have made the Lord their hope and confidence are "*... like a tree planted along a riverbank, with roots reaching deep into the water, its leaves staying green, always producing luscious fruit.*"[6] We need to have faith that is steady and strong like the snow that "*never melts up high in the Lebanon mountains;*" like the "*cold, flowing streams from crags of Mount Hermon (that) never run dry*" for "*these can be counted on.*"[7]

After the prophet Habakkuk challenged God's authority, at one point he gained great spiritual insight in concluding, "*... the righteous will live by his faith!*"[8] Faith, to Habakkuk, was humble trust in God even when life looked dim. It was daily dependence on God and walking with Him moment by moment: "*Though the fig tree should not blossom and there be no fruit in the vines, though the yield of the olive should fail and the fields produce no food ... Yet I will exult in the Lord. I will rejoice in the God of my salvation*" (Habakkuk 3:17–18 NASB).

Lord, no matter what difficulties or heartaches life holds, You are wise and Your plan for each one of us is perfect. You love us greatly and are faithful to keep Your promises. May we be like that plant that is deeply rooted, trusting You at all times and in every circumstance, clinging tightly to the hope that is within us.

> *Therefore, as you have received Christ Jesus the Lord, so walk in Him, having been firmly rooted and now being built up in Him and established in your faith, just as you were instructed, and overflowing with gratitude ...*
> (Colossians 2:6–7 NASB)

October 2006

Epilogue:

My brother, Curtis Alvin Searfoss, died five weeks after this writing. He put up a valiant fight, but in the end, the cancer overtook his body before he could have the bone marrow transplant. Curt accepted the Lord in his hospital bed in his last days at the hospital. Praise God!

> *And we are not afraid, but are quite content to die, for then we will be at home with the Lord.* (2 Corinthians 5:8 LB)

41

KEVIN'S SEARCH FOR GOD

Kevin had been on my mind a lot over the past few months. He had been looking for a job for months after having graduated from college. I couldn't stop thinking, *If God could get a hold of Kevin, what a great servant for the Lord he would be.* Not only did he get his degree in communications, but he has always been so personable and likeable; he is a great conversationalist. He enjoys being with people and has an empathetic heart. Even when he was little, he never liked hurting people's feelings.

During the last three weeks, I had made the same prayer request of my Bible study partners: Pray for Kevin to find the right job, and for his relationship with the Lord to deepen and be evident in his life. So often I had prayed that a Christian peer would talk with Kevin about God, but lately, I kept hearing the response, "Why don't you?" I had spoken to Kevin in the past about his spiritual life. Was God urging me to continue?

That Sunday I told my husband that I wanted to drive down to Kevin's place to talk with him by myself and spend some one-to-one time with him. I called him in the morning and left a message on his machine, but when he called back around noon, he said he was already in town at a friend's house and would come by a little later.

Once he arrived, we sat down and ate lunch. I wasn't sure how to start this important conversation, but after lunch, while we were still at the table, Kevin and I started talking, and everything evolved quite naturally, as if it were meant to be. We were so engrossed in conversation that George got up after a while and left the two of us to carry on while he read the newspaper in the living room.

Kevin brought up many of the same questions I remembered being in a quandary about before I finally relinquished myself to Christ at the age of thirty-five. Several times he stated, "The Bible is just a bunch of fairy tales!" He commented that the prophets and writers of the Bible were just writing stories that anyone could have written. "How do we know they are true?" he queried. "Jesus could have just been an imposter! Why don't we see miracles today like the parting of the Red Sea? Do you really believe Christ is coming back and only taking believers with Him?"

I did my best to field the questions, all the while making silent pleas to God to help me say things that would help him. I explained that all the words in the Bible were inspired by God; that the numerous writers of the Bible (forty, to be exact) wrote down only the messages God gave them. I said, "Even though the Bible was written over a thousand-year span, these men's words do not contradict each other. In fact, all the words blend together with one theme and into one harmonious story."

I continued further to emphasize that no matter how difficult it was to understand God's ways, the obvious fact that my life had changed when I accepted Christ as my personal Savior was a reality that could not be ignored. God's Spirit was alive in me. I was a new and different person, and I had felt His personal touch. I had witnessed His work in my life, even writing these incidents down over the years so I would not forget them. These were "God-incidences," not coincidences. I had experienced them. God was still in the business of miracles if we had eyes to see them.

I repeated several times to Kevin, "God's Word is alive and active." Continuing, I mentioned that many times I would be reading the Bible and would encounter just the right message, the exact words I needed to hear for that moment. Even though I had read the same passage before, new messages would jump out at me and I'd find myself saying in amazement, "I never noticed those words before!"

Then I added, "And you can't ignore the numerous prophesies that have come true."

I ran upstairs to get a copy of *The Living Bible* (which is easier to understand than other versions) and read Isaiah 53. It was written seven hundred years before Christ and described aspects of his death exactly as they occurred. I read a few proverbs and tabbed some pages for Kevin to read on his own. Actually, I had thought of Kevin often when reading the proverbs lately, thinking to myself, *I wish Kevin could read these wise words.* And maybe now he would. I prayed that he would.

I knew that the book of 1 John was a great place to begin a Bible journey, so I flipped to that book to tab the first page for Kevin. As I was flipping the pages, I happened to glance at one particular page that I had previously starred, and in that instant, the words "fairy tales" caught my attention. I started reading Peter's words, one page before 1 John: *"For we have not been telling you fairy tales when we explained to you the power of our Lord Jesus Christ and his coming again."* [1] *Wow!* I thought. *Thank you, Lord, for proving your living power through Your Word right here and right now!*

I ran down the hall to find Kevin, who was now in the laundry room. Excitedly, I began reading 2 Peter 1:16 and continued to the end of the first chapter, verse 21, realizing as I proceeded just how very timely and perfect all these precious words were for his ears at this moment.

> *For we have not been telling you fairy tales when we explained to you The power of our Lord Jesus Christ and his coming again. My own eyes have seen his splendor and his glory: I was there on the holy mountain when he shone out with honor given him by God his Father; I heard that glorious, majestic voice calling down from heaven, saying, 'This is my much-loved Son; I am well-pleased with him.'*
>
> *So we have seen and proved that what the prophets said came true. You will do well to pay close attention to everything they have written, for, like lights shining into dark corners, their words help us to understand many things that otherwise would be dark and difficult. But when you consider the wonderful truth of the prophet's words, then the light will dawn in you souls and Christ the*

Morning Star will shine in your hearts. For no prophecy recorded in Scripture was ever thought up by the prophet himself. It was the Holy Spirit within these godly men who gave them true messages from God.[2]

If I had searched and searched, I could not have found a more pertinent passage for Kevin to hear than this passage I "happened" to stumble upon! So true is the statement made by Ann Graham Lots: "When He speaks, it's in a language of our own lives, through a verse or passage of Scripture that just seems to leap off the page with our name on it"[3]—in this case, Kevin's name. I think Kevin was affected by this "happenstance" too. He left with the Bible atop his laundry basket of clean clothes.

Kevin, open your heart to your loving Savior who is reaching out to you. Believe He is real and can work in your life. You just witnessed His mighty power. You don't have to comprehend it all; just have faith. That's what God desires. When you finally trust and believe, the Holy Spirit will help you understand. You will no longer have to search, for you will know with certainty, and you will be at peace.

Thank you, Lord. May Kevin continue his quest for You and meet You personally. Don't let anyone or anything stand in his way.

February 2007

42

TRUTH MARCHES ON REGARDLESS OF DOUBT

When I talked to my son, he was angry because I wouldn't budge on my position in who Christ is (Lord and Savior) and what He has done for all of us, including Kevin. Kevin argued, "I just can't have faith in something that I believe is the biggest scam ever invented to control people's minds, implementing false hope on a belief that someone had two thousand years ago ... you can't attach facts to fairy tales!" (And this was just seven months after the last fairytale accusation!). Apparently he had seen something on the history channel about the Israelites eating some kind of mind-altering mushrooms that most likely made them hallucinate about seeing the miraculous parting of the Red Sea. And because it was on the history channel, he accepted that as historical truth.

He stated, "If I had a book that proved absolutely you are wrong in your beliefs, I bet you wouldn't even read it!" My first reaction was to think, *Why would I go out of my way to try and prove that what Christ said was fallible?* I know what He's personally done for me and how my life changed when He removed my sin and gave me the indwelling of His Holy Spirit. I thought, *I may not understand everything, but I'm not going to give up what I do know and what I have found in my personal relationship with Christ for what I don't know or totally understand.*

Kevin, you are not alone in your questions and confusion. There have been many who have doubted Christ's message; some individuals have been vehemently opposed to Christ but then, at some point, have surrendered their will to Christ and embraced Him as their Lord and Savior. Then their lives changed dramatically. This is true even of people who knew Jesus intimately, traveled with him, or were related to him. For instance, Jesus rebuked His own disciples for their unbelief: *"O unbelieving generation ... how long shall I put up with you?"*[1]

After Christ's death and resurrection, when Mary Magdelene reported to the disciples that she have seen Jesus alive, *"they refused to believe it."*[2] Even though Jesus had told them He would be crucified and three days later He would rise, they all still dismissed Mary, for *"these words appeared to them as non-sense, and they would not believe them."*[3]

Even Jesus' half brothers *"were not believing in Him"*[4] during His life that He was the Son of God, and they continually tried to dissuade Him from a path they considered insane: *"He has lost His senses."*[5] Jesus faced the same unbelieving opposition with the doubting chief priests, scribes, and elders, who constantly found fault with what He said and did. Prophesy had come true for these men because *"while seeing they did not see and while hearing they did not hear or understand ... their hearts had become dull."*[6] Truth was staring these men in the face, and they did not accept it in their pride and self-righteousness.

Festus, the Roman procurator of Judaea in AD 60, typifies a common reaction of some people today upon first hearing about Christ and His message for all humanity: *"... you are out of your mind!"*[7] In their human rationale, they conclude that the gospel message must be a fairy tale, something concocted to appease the masses, much too unbelievable to be true. Satan loved to promote that kind of thinking, especially with the younger generation, causing them to reject God's absolute authority and replace it with each individual's own perception of truth, encouraging them to live without fear of consequences.

Just because people doubt doesn't mean God's truth is not real. Even though others may foolishly condemn the Bible, that doesn't mean it is not God-inspired. Even though movies are produced and fictional books are written that refute the gospel, it doesn't mean God's Word is not true. It is their opinion, their viewpoint, and usually their goal is monetary in creating controversy.

Everyone can tell me I'm foolish to believe what they consider nonsense, but if I have experienced God's living power myself, nothing said can alter that reality. Something *that* life-changing and long-lasting is not something I willed to happen myself. It is God turning my life around for good and Christ living in me. Apostle Paul understood this when he said, *"I know very well how foolish it sounds to those who are lost when they hear that Jesus died to save them. But we who are saved recognize this message is the very power of God."*[8]

How can this same major change happen to so many Christians and it just be called a fairy tale? What's unbelievable to me is that outside observers can't see God's hand in those life-altering experiences of others, or if they do see it, they refuse to believe it. Why would anyone fight God who just wants a personal relationship with each individual that will last through eternity? Why would anyone not want the peace and contentment that comes from knowing that he or she is loved unconditionally and saved? Why would anyone resist God's goodness, His grace, and forgiveness? Now, that's hard to believe!

God is good and, thank goodness, much wiser than us. He says, *"If you seek me with all your heart, you will find me,"*[9] and that came true for many—the disciples, Jesus' brothers—and continues to come true today for believers everywhere. "Not only is Christ mighty to save (Isaiah 63:1) those who repent, but He is able to make men repent. He can give them new hearts enabling them to believe,"[10] says Charles Spurgeon, nineteenth-century British preacher. "He is mighty to make the man who hates holiness love it and to constrain the despiser of His name to bend the knee before Him."[11]

What happened to Saul (Paul) in the Bible is a perfect example. Saul was not looking for an encounter with Jesus Christ; in fact, he was set on persecuting followers of Christ. God's Spirit entered into Saul's life dramatically, in a totally life-changing experience. Saul's salvation began with God initiating a divine contact. John 3:8 says, *"Just as you can hear the wind, but can't tell where it comes from and where it will go next, so it is with the Spirit. We do not know on whom He will next bestow this life from heaven."*[12] Like Paul, *"For those who are in opposition, perhaps God may grant them repentance leading to the knowledge of truth."*[13]

There is an old saying, "Seeing is believing." However, with Jesus, the opposite is true. In believing, we see for ourselves God's living power. God's Spirit is alive and active in every believer. His Word is alive for anyone who reads it with an open, trusting heart. *"You love him even though you have never seen him, though not seeing him, you trust him ..."*[14] In this case, *believing* is seeing! And once that happens, there is no doubt.

So, my precious Kevin, I will never give up pleading with God that by His mercy and grace, and by the power of His Spirit, He will turn your heart around to Him. Do not become so dull and hardened that you refuse to see truth, desire it, or accept it. I pray God will continue to watch over you and draw you close so that you will come to know the truth of His love for yourself.

Lord, I know I cannot control the outcome of my children's lives. They are in your hands. I trust in the plans You have for them. I thank you for what You are going to do. You are in control, and You, indeed, are "mighty to save."

September 2007

43

ONE PATHWAY OF TRUTH

It was New Year's Day, and a good friend, Jean, who I had known since childhood and had lived in my same neighborhood, was in town visiting. It was always great seeing her even though her out-of-state move had made that happen less frequently. As we sat in the living room amid the holiday disarray (I was in the middle of putting decorations down), we got caught up on personal news.

I was surprised to find out that Jean had become reacquainted with an old high school boyfriend after finding him online. I could tell she was excited to be e-mailing this old flame and mentioned that she had actually seen him in person on one of her visits. She was filling me in on all the details, saying they just clicked and could easily talk on the phone for hours. She proceeded to explain that they even shared the same religious belief that there are many pathways to God.

I was stunned! Had I heard correctly? Jean had gone to a Christian high school and I used to accompany her sometimes when she attended services and programs at a local Christian church. What was this all about? When had she suddenly acquired this all-inclusive universal viewpoint?

I didn't say anything to her, but inwardly I was stunned. What had happened? I knew one couldn't be a Christian and also believe that all pathways lead to God. Just that morning I had written down some Scriptures after doing my Beth Moore Bible study on the disciple John. I remembered it saying: *"If we say we have no sin, we are deceiving ourselves and the truth is not in us,"*[1] and *"if we say that we have not sinned, we make Him (Christ) a liar and His word is not in us."*[2]

From personal experience, hadn't I tried various means to draw near to God and know Him personally, finding out that it came only through humbling myself, believing, and receiving His Son's sacrifice for my sins? It was such an amazing moment the first time I *knew,* without a doubt, that God and I had connected in a personal way; and that came about only because my sins were removed "as far as east is from the west."[3]

A particular Bible verse at that time became such a blessing to me: *"They shall **know** Me from the least of them to the greatest of them, saith the Lord: for I will forgive their iniquities and will remember their sins no more.*[4] This verse was such a reassurance to me. It meant that because I *knew* God personally now, with the help of His Holy Spirit living in me (*"The Father will send the Helper, the Holy Spirit, who will teach you all things ..."*[5]), my sins were completely gone—blotted out, as if they had never existed! I could *not* know God intimately and with certainty, as I did, if my sins still remained.

I wanted to speak to Jean about all of this, but it needed to be the right time, and God needed to do the speaking through me. So, I prayed and waited for direction. It didn't take long. Thursday morning I settled into my chair at my desk with my hot tea, prepared to diligently finish my study for that week to be ready for the discussion that night. I always looked forward to my quiet time with God and awaited His presence expectantly. It was definitely exciting to see how God speaks personally through His Word, and that day was no different.

I started reading Beth Moore's words: "Satan does all he can to keep us lost and blinded to truth. He knows we are created with a longing for God that we often confuse with a longing for spiritual things."[6] She continued to state that spiritually hungry individuals could still have a belief system involving God, but deny their only access to God, which is through Jesus Christ's torn flesh, adding, "To deny His incarnation is to deny our only means of salvation."[8]

The next statement almost made me jump: "You may know someone who is spiritual, but who doesn't believe in Christ's incarnate death and resurrection as the means to salvation."[9] The author then asked the reader to describe that belief system. (This was no coincidence! It had my friend's name written all over it!) Thinking of Jean, I wrote, "It's a more universal belief that there are many pathways to God (through

Jesus, Mohammed, Buddha, being good, etc.). With this premise, good works is the basis of salvation, not Christ's sacrifice on the cross for our sins."

I knew I hadn't read this particular lesson just for my benefit. It was meant to be read by my friend. It became very clear that the relevancy of other verses in John's first epistle also needed to be shared with her:

> *We have seen and testify that the Father has sent the Son to be the Savior of the world.* (1 John 4:14 NASB)

> *The Son of God appeared for this purpose, to destroy the works of the devil.* (3:8b)

> *He who has the Son has the life; he who does not have the Son of God does not have the life.* (5:12)

It was obvious that Satan was still hard at work undermining the critical issue of salvation, feeding not only my friend but also the whole world with a lie. I felt certain that through God's Word by means of this Bible study, God was wooing Jean back to the one pathway of truth: *"For there is one God, and one mediator also between God and men, the man Christ Jesus, who gave Himself as a ransom for all."*[10] I decided to copy several pages of my study and give them to her, and pray that she would be receptive.

Thank you, Lord. You sent your precious Son to show us Your loving and merciful plan for our redemption. You tell us in Your Word that *"if we confess our sins, (You) are faithful and righteous to forgive our sins and cleanse us from all unrighteousness."*[9] You are so wise to devise such an uncomplicated, foolproof way to make us all acceptable in your sight. It just takes simple faith to believe. You did all the work. Thank you for loving us, in all our waywardness, as much as You do. You are the way, the truth, and the life.[11]

January 2008

44

THE SALVATION EXPERIENCE

It is both fascinating and awe-inspiring how God makes contact differently and uniquely for every person in the salvation experience. Paul, for example, went from persecuting Christians to suddenly being confronted by God on the Damascus road and becoming one of the most devoted disciples of Christ. Then there was the divinely appointed meeting of the Ethiopian eunuch, riding in his chariot while reading Scripture that he didn't understand, and Philip, who willingly explained it to him and baptized him because the eunuch believed that Jesus Christ was the Son of God.

John MacArthur said that God is sovereign in salvation. It begins with a "divine, sovereign contact." However, for Paul and the Ethiopian, isn't it amazing how all the pieces fit to make that contact become a reality? We can witness that same reality in the stories of many born-again Christians. I saw the proof of that divine encounter in the testimonies of some Christians I know. Here are just a few of those "born again" experiences, each one unique and different.

Paula was the oldest of three girls in the family, and because of that, she tried to live up to her mother's expectation of being a good example to her younger sisters. Even though her parents did not consistently go to church, she and one of her sisters would walk down the street to attend a local church a couple times a week. One day when she was ten and listening to the minister, he said that if a person hadn't made a personal invitation to ask Christ into his or her life, that person would not go to heaven. As Paula stated, "I was shocked!" Being such a conscientious child, she had always believed her good deeds were enough. So that day, upon arriving home from church, she went into her room and, by herself, prayed and invited Christ to be her Savior. Her new life in Christ began at that moment.

Leslie said she accepted Jesus as her Savior when she was seventeen years old and a junior in high school. She grew up going to church with her family on Christmas and Easter, received her first Holy Communion and confirmation in the church, but did not have a personal relationship with the Lord. Her little sister of seven asked if she would go with her to a small church that was starting in the living room of a neighbor's house because the pastor's son (who was in her sister's class at school) had said she would get extra Sunday school points if she brought someone. There, Leslie said she learned about how much God and Jesus loved her no matter what she did. This was very important, especially since her parents argued and fought with each other all the time and took out their anger and frustration on her, and she grew up thinking it was all her fault. Through this small church, she came to know God's unconditional love. She couldn't get over the fact that, as she stated, "Jesus left heaven, the most wonderful place you can imagine, to come to earth and die for me. Even if I was the only one on earth, Jesus died for me ... He loves me!" Leslie's three younger sisters and brother eventually accepted Jesus as their Lord and Savior too.

Denise was raised in the church and went to tent meetings but didn't have a "born again" experience until she was two weeks away from delivering her first child. She was twenty-six and had been given a set of Bible study tapes on "God's Plan for the Wife and Mother." The audio teacher gave example after example of how she had asked God for specific help with her children and had received specific answers. Denise had never known that kind of two-way conversation with God, and she began praying to God for that kind of personal relationship. She stated, "That was the defining moment in my life." Soon after, she was moved to take an in-depth Bible study and through that experience testified, "Jesus became everything to me, and God started answering my prayers."

Laura said that when she was forty-four, she found herself alone at home more often than ever before. Her husband was working a lot of overtime, and her children were getting older and spending more time with their friends. She confided, "I went into depression and had great emptiness," but she didn't realize that was the problem, and none of her doctors could figure out physically what was wrong with her. Finally a psychiatrist suggested she take medicine—"something like Prozac." The second day she took it, she said, "I can't do this" and threw the medicine away. Laura continued, "I didn't understand I was being led by the Holy Spirit," but one day, "I went down to the floor and gave my life to the Lord because I had screwed it all up!" Things changed from then on. God gave her a desire to read His Word (which she had not done before) "sometimes up to three hours a day!" He also started opening her eyes to a series of things: what was happening to our country, and the true condition of her heart. (She had always done things her way before). She is so grateful to be born again and have this new life in Christ.

I grew up going to church, but even as an adult attending church and going to Bible Studies, I realized that God didn't seem real to me. I was searching with all my heart but was not relinquishing self, and it wasn't until my dad died and I was thirty-five, carrying my third child, that I followed the suggestion in a minister's sermon to stand in front of a mirror and humbly cup my hands in front of me and repeatedly say, "God, take all that I'm not and put it into all that you are." As I said that over and over, I saw how small I was compared to God Almighty, how unworthy I was, and how desperately I needed Him. I remember just crying and crying, relinquishing control. From that point on, my life was different. I knew that God loved me, that He was real, and that He had reached out to save me. I had such a newfound desire to read the Bible. I just couldn't seem to get enough of it! I actually understood it for the first time. Now with His Spirit in me, I was viewing everything through His eyes, seeing everything in a different light. I became more and more aware of God's daily presence in my life, and my focus totally changed.

All this helped me to see that God makes contact when He decides, and that no two experiences are alike. For Paul, the Spirit of God was

The Salvation Experience

preparing him all his life to bring him to this critical "born again" moment. I think seeing Stephen being stoned to death and hearing him ask God to forgive his transgressors must have affected Paul greatly. God uses all methods—some dramatic, and some evolving over a period of time—to bring someone to the point of salvation.

It has also become more apparent to me how important it is for *us* to do our part to help make all those pieces fit that God planned from the beginning of time. God designed our lives and the pathways we should follow beforehand. In the Bible, He says He will be faithful to complete a good work in us,[1] but it takes our cooperation. We must bend and be willing participants, keeping our ears and eyes open, quietly listening to His voice—not only for ourselves, but for others as well.

Maybe we can be a Philip and offer clarification on the Bible, or be a Stephen and show Christian love and forgiveness. Maybe we can encourage someone to attend church or a Bible study so he or she can hear God speak through His Word, or maybe we can give someone just the right tapes on a topic or a Scripture verse. Possibly, just being a good Christian example or showing contagious joy would be the impetus for someone desiring the same for himself or herself. We must work together with God in building His kingdom. We may not even be aware of times when we have been instruments in God's hands to affect eternity for others.

Dear Jesus, may we all be open and available servants saying "I am here, Lord."

February 2009

45

A HEART FOR GOD

Written to my Lord on Valentine's Day:

Let the heart of those who seek the Lord be glad.
—1 Chronicles 16:10 (NASB)

Oh God, our Father, precious Savior, Lord of all heaven and earth, worthy and wondrous, accept the feeble words of my grateful heart this day. You are holy and perfect, complete in compassion—so merciful. The length of Your long-suffering is unfathomable, Your loving-kindness never-ending. I love You. I adore You. I cannot thank You enough, my blessed Lord. You are purity, righteousness, Lord of all fairness. You lift me above the disturbance of discontent, the wrangling of resentment, the crankiness of complaints. My heart sings praises of Your wondrous acts: jewels of grace dazzling brilliantly to those who have eyes to see them. Lord of peace, who brings the end of envy, strife, and hatred, You make the wolf live with the lamb, the leopard lie down with the young goat, the lion and calf graze together,[1] none desiring the proud necessity of conquest or power, but living in harmony with gentle spirits. All creation unites in shouting "Hallelujah," "All to Thee," and "I surrender all," to the almighty One, who is so deserving. My affection pours forth in a torrent of adulation. Glory to You! My heart sings its praises; may it always be.

Valentine's Day is all about love, and of course, I think of my love for my husband, family, and friends; but I also think about God's great love for me. Love is the main topic of the Bible, in which it is written about more than anything else. Apostle Paul says that love *"satisfies all of God's requirements. It is the only law you need."*[2] Love is the essence of life, the foundation, and the purpose. It's the greatest gift of all!

> *But now faith, hope, love, abide these three; but the greatest of these is love.* (1 Corinthians 13:13 NASB)

The Greatest Gift

If I had a mighty faith well-grounded in the truth,
believing I could speak and even make a mountain move,
it would gain me nothing; what good would my faith be
without love to show why God bestowed this gift on me.

If I took all that I owned and gave it to the poor,
if I prided myself on what I do for the Lord,
what would I gain in the end, doing all this good
if it hadn't love behind it, as God said it should?

If I spoke all languages in heaven and on earth,
if I had the gift of tongues as God's ambassador,
I'd just be a clanging symbol or a noisy gong
if I did not show my love for others all along.

If I knew all things, and the future I could see,
if God blessed me with the wondrous gift of prophesy,
knowing all God's mysteries would be a meaningless call
if God's love for others was not seen in me at all

If I taught and preached God's Word, surrendering my life
even to the point of death, being burned alive,
nothing would I profit sacrificing for God's Son
without love for others, the main reason it was done.

All the gifts of God will pass away some future day.
Prophesy and tongues and knowledge will be done away.
Now I see in part, but someday I'll see God above,
realizing the greatest gift remaining, will be love.

    February 14, 2010

46

A Memorable Musical Moment

After fifty-seven years of living on her own in the same house, the time had finally come when my eighty-nine-year-old mother could no longer take care of herself. We had tried over that last summer to keep her in her home, getting outside help for her several days a week and spending more time assisting her ourselves. But after a few more car dents, food that had been prepared and left untouched in the refrigerator, and other oddities like finding the garage door opener in the toaster, it was obvious that Mom needed more consistent care.

We visited several assisted senior arrangements and finally selected one nearby. It was a big step for Mom to leave her home, with all its personal possessions and cherished memories, and move into a single bedroom. I was optimistic, however, knowing that Mom was outgoing and garrulous. I felt she would meet some new ladies and participate in social activities.

Unfortunately, soon after her move, she declined quickly and her dementia became even more prevalent. Mom, too, was becoming more and more aware of her inability to think clearly and carry on a simple conversation. Each day, she became more reclusive and depressed, turning into a totally different person than the mother I once knew.

It was only seven months into her stay there when she was taken to the hospital for what turned out to be a bladder and kidney infection. After her five-day stay, she was released back to the skilled nursing section for more medical care. To our surprise, she was now spending all her time in a wheelchair. It was most discouraging to visit her and also see all the other residents there so helpless and sad. After leaving, I would ask God to help me know what to do to help lift her spirits, to give her even a few moments of joy.

Since it was summer, I had a little more time on my hands, and I decided to use those hands to brush up on my neglected piano playing. Mom had always loved music and was the instigator for my lifelong love of music. She had always enjoyed hearing me play the piano.

There was one piece of music in particular that had been a favorite of hers and mine—"Clair de Lune" by Debussy. I had played it at a piano recital and had also performed it at our church for my grandmother's memorial service. It was one of those pieces that, even as an adult, I would get out and play occasionally when I got into my infrequent piano-playing moods. I decided that this would be the perfect song to play for Mom. However, when I went digging through the piano bench archives, the music was nowhere to be found. So I made a special trip to the music store to buy another copy. Once it was in my possession, I practiced diligently every day for about three weeks.

The day finally came when I visited Mom armed with "Clair de Lune" and several other pieces. I wheeled Mom right up in front of the grand piano in the large room used for church and other social gatherings at the senior facility, which was empty at the time. It was very peaceful—just the two of us. I sat down and played uninterrupted for about half an hour. Mom sat listening intently as the notes echoed off the walls. It made me feel so blessed to hopefully give her even a little ray of sunshine with this private mini-concert.

During this time when Mom was in skilled nursing, I was also agonizing over what should be done about her future living arrangement. I didn't think she really needed to remain there, and yet she was not independent enough to go back into the group home area. She hadn't seemed to fare well with the last move. I thought maybe it would be better for her to stay put and not make too many changes at her age.

Just about that time, a friend of mine was moving her mother into a private assisted living home near us that had one bedroom available. After visiting the residence, I felt Mom would maybe do better in this

A Memorable Musical Moment

more personal homey environment; plus, she would once again have her own room, and she'd be closer to us. I stressed over having to make these decisions, asking, "Lord, guide me. Help me know if this is what I should do."

A few days later, the decision was made and we moved Mom into her new living quarters. I helped her get settled and stayed to visit with her and the other four residents as they sat around the kitchen table finishing their after-dinner juice. All of a sudden, my ears perked up while I was listening to the music playing in the background. Was that really what I thought it was? As I strained to hear every note, there was no mistake; the sweet sound of "Clair de Lune" filled the kitchen. In my whole life I had never heard that song played on the radio, a CD, or even at a live performance (except my own!). The timing was incredible! In my excitement, I kept repeating over and over, "Mom, that's 'Clair de Lune!' Can you believe that's 'Clair de Lune'?"

I think everyone there must have thought I was the one needing the extra care, but somehow, right at that moment, I knew God was present and letting me know (in only the way that God can) that everything was okay and that this was where my mother should be; He was giving me peace about my decision. This little musical moment was no coincidence.

Thank You, Lord, for giving me this glimpse of Your glorious compassion and love. Thank You for showing me that You hear me and that You are always right by my side. Thank You for walking with me and helping me see that I can cast all my anxiety on You because You care for me.[1] All praise to You, my most wonderful, blessed Lord.

And the peace of God, which transcends all understanding, will guard your hearts and your minds in Christ Jesus.
(Philippians 4:7 NASB)

August 2010

47

LET THE CHILDREN COME TO ME

So often throughout my life, I have prayed that my family, friends, and people all over the world will come to know Jesus as their Lord and Savior. If Jesus is (as He called Himself) *"the Lord, in charge of the harvest,"*[1] and if He decides who *"he will next bestow this life from heaven,"*[2] why were more people not being saved? If God is Creator of the universe, is good, and loves us, why couldn't He make that happen? What was causing the impasse?

As I was recently reading through the gospel of Luke, I discovered a couple passages that really caught my attention; somehow I felt they were at the crux of the matter. I had read Luke several times before, but for the first time, these verses stood out as though I had never read them before. Was God focusing me on these verses for a reason? Was it important that I receive the impact and significance of their truths at this very moment in time?

Both passages had to do with children, and both basically conveyed the same message. And when Jesus says something twice, it's always done for good reason (NLT):

> *Jesus said, "O Father, Lord of heaven and earth, thank you for hiding these things (the Truth) from those who think themselves wise and clever, and for revealing them to the childlike. Yes, Father, it pleased You to do it this way."* (Luke 10:21)

LET THE CHILDREN COME TO ME

> *Jesus said to His disciples who thought the little children were bothering Him, "Let the children come to me. Don't stop them! For the Kingdom of God belongs to those who are like these children. I tell you the truth, anyone who doesn't receive the Kingdom of God like a child will never enter it."* (Luke 18:16–17)

These Scriptures didn't have so much to do with children, per se, as they did to the importance of individuals having a "childlike" attitude in approaching God and trusting what He says. I decided to look up the word "childlike" in *Webster's New World Dictionary* to see exactly what that word meant. They listed words such as open, genuine, sincere, honest, unassuming, unsuspicious, simple, unworldly, unpretending, credulous (easily convinced), believing, and trusting. Wow! I thought, *That's how God wants us to be; we are to come to Him from a position of dependency, need, and obedience, not one of cynicism, doubt, or self-sufficiency.*

What God wanted *most* was for us to have a pure and simple acceptance of Him, like children have toward adults on whom they depend. In that childlike trusting attitude, we acknowledge that God, Maker of heaven and earth, knows better than we do. We don't analyze, dissect, or put up defenses. We don't question at every turn of events, asking "How come?" or "Why?" or "Why not?" Our first reaction isn't "That's illogical," or "That's not fair!"

We willingly accept and trust that God is good, He is wise, and it is *His* plan. He's just seeing if we are willing to bend our knee to Him, even if things don't seem plausible in our minds. As Jesus stated in Luke 10:21, God hides *"these things from those who think themselves wise and clever ..."* Our compliance shows our proper alignment with Him: contrite, humbled, obedient, and awestruck.

God put it in our laps. He's in charge, but He didn't make us puppets. He wants our genuine love, not a forced affection. God is constantly wooing, saying "Come to me like a child." But we have been given free will to choose. Is it God's way or what we think it should be? God wants us to take that step of faith toward Him with open arms, accepting and believing. That simple childlike trust is the condition of the heart that God is looking for; that's what God will respond to, and it is what He desires. The Bible says, *"Yet to all who received him, to those who believe in his name, he gave the right to become children of God."*[3]

I had a chance to experience this childlike attitude in presenting the gospel message to a group of fourth- and fifth-grade children in a public school as part of an after-school program that I teach. We had talked about how God had created this beautiful world for us to enjoy, and created us to have a loving relationship with Him. I pointed out that unfortunately, man's selfishness and ego (sin) formed a barrier between man and God in the past and continues to do so today. I explained to them that man is incapable of breaking that barrier himself, so in order for us to be acceptable in God's eyes and not be separated from Him forever, God sent His Son to earth to take that barrier of sin upon Himself and die on the cross in our place. All we have to do is believe what Jesus did for us to save us, receive this gift of salvation, and we will be with God now and forever.

I told them that God wanted to keep it simple. He wanted everyone, from little two-year-old children up to elderly people in their nineties, to be able to easily receive salvation. He wanted people from different countries, speaking different languages, looking different, all to be able to come to Him. He did not want anyone to have to pass a test. (What if some of them failed?) God just wanted people to say, "I believe you, Lord; I'm sorry for the wrong things I have done, and I want to receive you in my heart." So easy on our part!

The children listened intently. They were interested in understanding God's plan. They did not want to be separated from God. They accepted it without question and believed what Jesus Christ had done to bring them back to God and make them acceptable to Him.

I then asked those who wanted to receive Christ as their personal Savior to repeat the invitation prayer after me. As far as I could tell, every child participated. They were so eager to repeat what I said that they started talking before I even had a chance to finish each of my sentences. They understood that they had nothing to lose and everything to gain with this simple acceptance on their part. They weren't afraid to walk forward in faith to discover truth for themselves, and they trusted it would happen.

God loves our family members, our friends, and everyone in the world even more than we do. He created them, and His Son died for them. God's concern for their salvation is even greater than our concern. He is working in them every day, trying to draw them to Him, wanting a personal relationship with them, pleading, "Come … come to me."

Lord, I pray that in this complex world of concreteness and calculating minds, people will realize that You give a gift of grace that comes with no conditions and needs no further clarification. You just ask for simple, uncluttered trust. Oh, Lord, enable my family, my friends, and people everywhere to have that open and eager childlike faith. I know they will find You. Help them to hear Your voice today.

Let the Children Come to Me

>With their hearts and eyes they see.
>Come to Me, come to Me.
>They accept, they believe;
>without question, they receive.
>Come to Me, come to Me.
>
>Simple gift they take from Me—
>the gift of life eternally.
>No stumbling blocks do they construct;
>they're open wide with childlike trust.
>Come to Me, come to Me.
>
>They do not think that they're above
>God, Creator, Lord of Love.
>Jesus Christ they want to please.
>God's kingdom belongs to these.
>Come to Me, come to Me.

Those who think they're clever and wise,
God hides the truth, no compromise.
For the truth to be revealed,
become a child; you'll find it's real.

The Spirit and the bride say, "Come." Let each one who hears them say the same, "Come." Let the thirsty one come – anyone who wants to; let him come and drink the water of Life without charge. (Revelation 22:17 LB)

November 2010

48

I Understand

My year's Bible study in Kings and Chronicles was coming to an end. In a way, I was relieved because the lessons seemed like a vicious cycle: the Jewish people's fickleness and failings, their constant falling away from obeying God, and then God either punishing them or mercifully restoring them. God's frustration in dealing with His beloved chosen ones was evident on every page.

For some reason, pondering about this latest Bible study made me think of Adrian, the thirty-year-old niece of one of my friends. She was moving back home again with her parents because her latest job of three months had not worked out and her roommate had left. This was not the first time she had moved back home (or had lost her job). Even though she had lots of loving support from her parents, and great potential for success, she kept repeating the same pattern of making bad decisions for her life which caused negative consequences. It seemed that she would try to make changes, but then she would revert back into her old habits, which obviously weren't working.

Once again, I was putting extra effort into praying for her. I knew her quite well and had watched her grow up. When someone you care about so much can't seem to find her or his way, or be disciplined enough to make needed changes, and you want so much to help that person, have you ever thought to yourself, *I wish I could just take charge of their body, for a while, for them!* As odd as that may sound, I have found myself wishing I could do this for Adrian. I know I'm far from perfect, but there are pearls of wisdom gained from years of experiencing life which would definitely be helpful in making sound decisions for Adrian, and in steering her in the right direction (if I had control of her body).

I've gone over in my mind what I would do. Here are a few of my ideas: stay physically fit, look neat, eat healthy food, read up on current events both local and worldwide, spend a big portion of the day job hunting, participate in groups to meet new people (hopefully, who would be a positive influence), and grow spiritually (most importantly). The list could go on: have follow-through, be consistent, think positive thoughts, try to become more organized, and not give up. Because I am a fairly self-disciplined and determined person, I think I could do these things by actually, being her. I felt strongly that these would definitely be positive steps for necessary change.

Suddenly it dawned on me—wasn't that God's answer to man's failings? It was obvious to me in reading the Old Testament that man, relying on his own devices, failed time and again to live up to God's expectations. Story after story related how people thought they knew better than God what was good for their lives, succumbing to outside influences and inward desires that were contrary to God's will and their best interest. They desperately needed to be saved from themselves! And the problem wasn't with just a few individuals, but everyone, then and now!

What was God to do? He had created people to love Him and have a perfect, unobstructed relationship with Him. Giving them the Ten Commandments and the law to follow had not changed their behavior. They constantly fell short of His standard of righteousness. Since God is by nature holy, pure, good, and without sin, He must have wept many times in this broken relationship because of man's sin, lamenting, "How can you, my beloved children, ever be acceptable in My sight? How can you get near to Me? I want to be with you now and forevermore, but I abhor sin; I can't abide it! *'How can we walk together with your sins between us?'*[1] I cannot commune with you unless it's removed, and I will be separated from you forevermore."

What was His perfect answer? He would replace our hearts of stone with hearts of flesh. He would give us a new heart and put a new spirit within us.[2] God would do what I wanted to do for Adrian. He would come live inside us. He would give us a part of Himself (His Spirit) to guide us and give us His wisdom, His insights, and His ability to fight the temptations of this world.

However, in order for God to dwell in our bodies, He would need a pure and holy container. How would that happen? God would send His Son, Jesus, to take our sins from us, all the wrongs we have ever done, and He would die the death we rightfully should experience ourselves because of our sin. Once that sin was removed from us, God's Holy Spirit would be free to move into our cleansed hearts, minds, and souls. As apostle Paul said, our body would become a living "temple of the Holy Spirit."[3]

What kindness and love were shown on God's part to give us this redemptive gift of life at the expense of His Son's suffering and death. Once saved, we would not be dictated by external laws and our inability to keep them to please God, but *"the Kingdom of God (would be) within us,"*[4] helping us want to do right and please Him. It is God's simple answer in bringing man to Himself and vice versa; yet many people want to make it so complicated.

This unbroken relationship doesn't just happen without our cooperation either. God wants us to choose, to make that decision that we need Him, that our sin separates us, and that God knows what He is doing in sending His Son to show us the way back to Him. We need to surrender, to relinquish, and to rely on a higher authority, not ourselves. "Jesus, Jesus, You are the answer," we need to say with our lips, and we must accept Him by faith in our hearts.

God's love for us is beyond our comprehension, higher than the highest heaven and deeper than the deepest ocean. His plan for our salvation is beautiful and perfect, this ultimate sacrifice in sending His own precious Son to save us. As explained in the Bible, *"He saved us, not on the basis of deeds* (and by our flawed efforts) ... *but according to His mercy, by the washing of regeneration, and renewing by the Holy Spirit."*[5] It's a gift of Himself.

With God's presence in us and with us at all times, we have God's strength and power to face and overcome any difficulty—everything that we are incapable of handling on our own. We have Christ within, bringing us the peace of God's eternal presence and the hope of all He saved us for and desires us to become.

Lord, thank You for helping me understand more fully why You chose this perfect plan for our salvation. For those who believe, we have Christ within, continually giving us Your insights, strength, power, and peace, which we so desparately need. Thank you for loving us so much and for blessing our lives.

May 2011

49

OUR PRAYERS LIVE ON

My small group of sewing friends had gathered on our last night of our summer Bible study. It had been a wonderful six weeks studying God's Word together, just the four of us. We were on the last chapter of our workbook on the importance of prayer. I knew, from many Scriptures I had read previously, how much God values our prayers. So many of them emphasized the importance and power of persistent prayer. What I read that night in our workbook about prayer, however, became even more significant to me because of some recent events with our family. It stated, "As we persevere in prayer, we combine faith and patience and place our hope in God. And while we wait, God is working."[1]

How many times over the years had I prayed for my family, that they would have a close relationship with God and that they would be certain of His presence. I knew God wanted that too, and that He had heard my prayers, for He even said through the prophet Isaiah, *"Before they call I will answer; while they are still speaking I will hear."*[2] And again, John the disciple reiterated that confidence when he stated, *"if we ask anything according to His will He hears us. And if we know that he hears us – whatever we ask - we know that we have what we asked of him."*[3]

That same evening of the Bible study, I had shared with the group about George's father, Cecil, who told me he prayed every day for our family when he was alive. I knew he prayed daily for his wife, Eva, too; and yet, even though Cecil's life revolved around his relationship with His Savior and with the Bible (his constant companion of many years),

Eva showed no interest in a similar pursuit. Cecil lived to be ninety-four, and he had prayed for her salvation a long time. Even on his deathbed he told me how much he loved Eva, and I knew how much he wanted her with him in heaven. All those prayers for Eva's salvation over the years had gone unanswered.

Over this last year, however, I witnessed a slow change in Eva. She was undergoing many physical and emotional problems: constant back pain, difficult breathing issues, nausea, chest pain, and extreme tiredness all the time. She had seen one doctor after another. Having no energy to do anything, she was discouraged and depressed. On top of that, because of her physical limitations, her daughter, Debbie, who has special needs and who had always lived with her, had been moved to another living arrangement. All her life, Eva had taken care of Cecil and Debbie, and now she felt useless and alone.

Surprisingly, Eva started reading a daily devotional book given to her by her sister called *Jesus Calling*. Much of the reading was about trusting God regardless of difficult circumstances, and the importance of resting in His loving presence even in the toughest of times. Eva had always seemed very self-sufficient, not needing to rely on anyone else. However, putting her faith in all the doctors and new medications was not giving her any relief. She was finally realizing her inability to cope with what was happening in her life and had told me that she was praying more and more each day that God would help her. Was God getting her to a point where she had nowhere else to look but up?

During this time when I was reading the Bible, I came across a couple verses that I felt were meant for Eva the moment I read them. They were both in Psalms, David's plea to God: *"O Lord, from the depths of despair I cry for your help. Hear Me! Answer! Help me! Lord, if you keep in mind our sins then who can get an answer to his prayers? But you forgive! What an awesome thing this is!"*[4] *"If I had cherished sin in my heart, the Lord would not have listened."*[5]

Eva was praying and crying out to God, but I was aware, just like David, that sin causes an obstruction in prayer; that in order for us to have an open channel to God, we need to confess our sins. Isaiah knew about this when he said, *"Look! Listen! God's arm is not amputated – he can still save. Gods ears are not stopped up – he can still hear. There's nothing wrong with God; the wrong is in you! Your wrongheaded lives caused the split between you and God. Your sins get between you so that he doesn't hear!"*[6]

For months I waited and prayed to find the right time to speak to Eva about these verses. The morning she was here visiting on George's sixty-second birthday, I felt the urgency to talk to her about them. We sat together on the couch at about 9:45 a.m., right before I was going to drive her back home. I was constantly praying for God's help, that He would do the speaking through me, that this was the right time. I was very aware that Eva had a mind of her own, and I didn't want anything to happen that would negatively impact our relationship. I also knew that this was Cecil's greatest desire for her (mine too), and with her ill health, opportunities were getting more limited. I would never forgive myself if something happened to her before I got a chance to talk with her again.

I decided to go ahead and read Psalms 66:15 and 130:3–4 to her. Then I simply asked her, "Do you believe that your sin separates you from God? Do you believe that Christ died for you?" Without hesitation, she responded, "Yes! Yes!" With God's Spirit in the lead, Eva repeated my words to invite Christ into her life. I was surprised at her complete willingness after so many years of resistance and disinterest. I felt that this was God's plan all along, and it was happening according to His timetable. I was so happy for her. That night I sent my kids this e-mail about the day's event:

> To my children,
>
> I just wanted to tell you the good news that this morning around 9:45 while I was talking with Grandma Speicher, she accepted Christ as her personal Savior. I felt an urgency to bring it up today and wasn't sure how she would respond to the invitation, but she didn't hesitate. I praise God that He has been working on softening her heart and that she was receptive to His call. Not only did we celebrate your dad's 62nd birthday today, but a new life in Christ!
>
> Love,
> Mom

Kim immediately responded, "That is great news! She will be seeing Grandpa in heaven when that time comes."

Yes, I believe all the angels in heaven were singing, and I'm sure Grandpa Speicher was too. Cecil's perseverance in prayer had been answered, even though it was after His death. It gave me such hope to realize for my own children, my future grandchildren, George, and extended family that God does not forget our prayers; not one slips past Him, and they are all in His safe keeping.

Psalm 56:8 explains that God collects our tears and preserves them in a bottle, recording each one in His book. If God does that with our sorrowful tears, how much more must He guard and keep account of our precious prayers for our loved ones! Our prayers continue to be in His possession and live on even after we are gone from this life. Like the author of our study said: "Even though we may not see all our prayers answered in our lifetime, remember that God saves them and may answer them after we're gone."[7] How comforting that is!

Thank You, Lord, for showing me what a difference our prayers can make even when I do not see immediate results. You do not want us to give up in praying. Unlike us, You see all and know all. Our prayers live on in Your perfect keeping, will, and timing.

September 2011

50

A Peaceful Passing

It was the Tuesday after Christmas and the caretakers at Mom's assisted living home had called an ambulance to have Mom taken to the hospital. After tests were done, the doctors indicated that she had congestive heart failure and kidney failure stage 4 (stage 5 would require dialysis). Mom was put on heart medication and antibiotics, but things did not look good. Because of Mom's serious condition, her age (ninety-one), her dementia, and because she had requested a directive in her will to not sustain life should recovery look dismal, the doctors, Nancy (my sister) and I made the decision for her go on hospice. The nurses would just try to keep her comfortable, giving her small doses of morphine.

Mom was allowed to go back to the familiar assisted living home for her remaining days. She arrived Tuesday night (along with her hospital bed), back in her room, surrounded by her family pictures and favorite music playing. Mom never complained of pain, and she seemed aware enough to know we were there.

On Saturday morning a hospice pastor arrived, a nice young man named Jim. He was very pleasant, and after spending time with Mom, he said she had responded to him with yeses and nos. At seven that night, Nancy and I went home for dinner, but before leaving, I kissed Mom on the forehead and said, "I love you, Mom." She responded weakly, "Thank you."

Later on that evening, around 9:45, we received a call came from one of the caretakers: "I think you should come back!" We headed to

Mom's residence, and when we saw her, we were stunned. Her skin had paled and her breathing was louder and more labored. She was staring straight up at the ceiling as if she were in a trance. It almost didn't look like the same person we had left just three hours earlier.

A few minutes after 10:00, Nancy and I both were at Mom's bedside, and we immediately started to pray. As we prayed, it was almost as if God's Spirit took control. Nancy was quietly telling Mom it was okay to leave and to relinquish herself to God. I was lifting Mom up and praising God, seeing heaven opening and sensing that God was saying to her, *"Well done, good and faithful servant."*[1] I was humbled and awed at the same moment, feeling God's overwhelming presence, as if He were speaking through us to give Mom words of comfort and peace. I knew that God was controlling everything that was happening as Mom's spirit was leaving her earthly body, and that He was embracing her spirit in heaven.

Mom stopped breathing a couple times for about thirty seconds, and the next time, she did not draw another breath. There was no anxiety, no resistance, no agitation, no pain, and no fear; just stillness and calm. I had such a feeling of peace, I cannot even begin to explain it. It was really an amazing moment. As we looked at Mom's lifeless body, we knew that it was just a shell; that her spirit was gone and now safely residing with almighty God, the Creator and sustainer of life, here and eternally. It was 10:30 p.m. when my mother, Helen Middaugh Searfoss, peacefully passed away. It happened very quickly, but God was merciful; her final earthly hours were not prolonged. I had such an overwhelming sense of gratefulness. All I could do was say over and over again, "Thank you, Lord, thank you, thank you, thank you."

When I look back on Mom's last few weeks, I realize now that toward the end, when she was not talking and had her head down most of the time, it was a sign. She must have known instinctively that she was dying. As it indicated in a helpful little hospice booklet that was given to us, with the knowledge that "Yes, I am dying," a person begins to withdraw from the world around him or her. That is the beginning of separation—going inside, where there is only room for one; evaluating one's self and one's life. Just as the booklet said, Mom was sleeping more, taking more naps, increasingly losing interest in eating, and not wanting or needing to communicate. This was happening weeks before she even went into the hospital. I had no idea, at the time, what this withdrawal from everything and everyone meant. My mom was preparing herself for death.

I am now at peace with the comforting realization that my mom does not have to struggle with her dementia anymore. I am sorry that her last couple years were so frustrating for her and that she could not communicate easily with family and friends. That naturally distanced her from others, and I know she was lonesome a lot of the time. She even said to me several times, "I need a friend." That always made me feel sad, because I knew how important her friends were to her all of her life. However, I know Mom lived a good life, and I thank God that her dementia didn't worsen into Alzheimer's. She always knew who George was and who I was, and I am grateful for that.

Some things that occurred to me after Mom's death are rather interesting family coincidences:

1. Mom went into the hospital on Wednesday, December 28, which was the birthday of my brother Curt, who died six years ago from leukemia.
2. Mom died on her mother's birthday, January 7.
3. Mom died at the same time that my dad died over twenty-five years before, at 10:30 p.m.

Lord, I know that the number of Mom's days here on earth was written in Your great book. She trusted You throughout this journey called life. Now that the end has come for her here, we have nothing left to do but cherish loving memories and celebrate, knowing she is in her new eternal home with You.

> ... *I am continually with You; You have taken hold of my right hand. You guide me with your counsel, and afterward you will take me into glory.* (Psalm 73:23–24 NASB)

January 2012

51

A LOUD VOICE

As I was reading the book of Revelation, I was coming across some revelations for myself that might seem insignificant to others but had great significance to me. In the Revelation of Jesus Christ, the apostle John is given truths by God, communicated through His angel, about "things which must soon take place …" (Rev. 1:1). When this communication occurred, God spoke with power and authority. Literally, it was *loud!*

Throughout Revelation, God's angels speak in "loud voice(s)." After all, they were speaking for God Himself. In fact, Revelation 22:16 even states, "I, Jesus, have sent My angel to testify to you these things for the churches." God's words of power and authority through these spirit messengers commanded attention. Man was to be silenced, to hear, and take heed. What particularly interested me was the unvarying use of the word "loud" to describe their voices, and how many times it appears in the Scriptures. Also, sometimes "one voice" is mentioned even though it refers to many angels (NASB).

> *And I saw a strong angel proclaiming with a **loud voice**, "Who is worthy to open the book and to break its seal?"* (5:2)
>
> *I heard the voice of many angels … saying with a **loud voice**, "Worthy is the Lamb …"* (5:11, 12)

A Loud Voice

*Then I looked and I heard an eagle (angel?) flying in midheaven, saying with a **loud voice**, "Woe, woe, woe to those who dwell on the earth ..." (8:13)*

*Then the seventh angel sounded; and there were **loud voices** in heaven saying, "The Kingdom of the world has become the kingdom of our Lord and of His Christ and He will reign forever and ever." (11:15)*

*Then I heard a **loud voice** in heaven saying, "Now the salvation and the power and the kingdom of our God and the authority of His Christ have come ..." (12:10–11)*

*And I saw another angel ... and he said with a **loud voice**, "Fear God, and give Him glory because the hour of His judgment has come ..." (14:6–7)*

*And another angel came out of the temple, crying out with a **loud voice** to Him who sat on the cloud, "Put in your sickle and reap, for the hour to reap has come ..." (14:15)*

*After these things I heard something like a **loud voice** of a great multitude in heaven, saying, "Hallelujah! Salvation and glory and power belong to our God." (19:1)*

*Then I saw an angel standing in the sun, and he cried out with a **loud voice**, saying to all the birds which fly in midheaven, "Come, assemble for the great supper of God." (19:17)*

There are more: Revelation 7:2; 10:1–3; 14:2–3; 14:9, 18; 16:1; 18:1–2; 19:6; and 21:3.

Why did this seemingly minor detail that these angels were speaking in loud voices make such an impact on me? From my own experience, I knew it wasn't that they were just speaking loudly; God's mighty power was being delivered through these messengers to bring down stout hearts, hopefully obliging those who had never acknowledged the God of the universe to reverence Him when they heard His voice.

The prophet Daniel experienced this loud voice after seeing a vision of God, describing *"the sound of his words like the sound of a tumult."*[1] The impact of this powerful voice left Daniel with no strength and his *"face to the ground."*[2]

I was drawn back to a time about twenty-five years ago when I encountered that loud voice personally. It wasn't through what one typically thinks of as an angel, but one who could be considered an angel of sorts, for he was delivering God's words. I was getting into my car after a weekly Bible study, completely overwhelmed with confusion and frustration, trying to digest something that had happened in the Old Testament which I just couldn't understand. It was a complete bafflement to me how God could operate this particular way, and I was having trouble accepting it.

I had been trying so hard to develop a personal connection with God that I very much wanted, but no matter my effort, it just always seemed elusive. I thought maybe I should just quit the Bible study. I didn't know if I was angrier at myself or God. As I started the engine of my car, the voice of a prominent local pastor came thundering out over the radio, enveloping the vehicle. It was so loud and powerful. I remember feeling almost paralyzed, hardly able to even breathe. Unbelievably, he was speaking on the very topic I was in such a quandary about when I had gotten into the car. I recognized this pastor's voice, and yet it had a volume, power, and authority that was beyond human, not like anything I had ever experienced before (and I had not turned the volume up!). It didn't take long for me to realize that God was speaking to me through this man. I remember feeling a solemn awe and reverence, also very small, at the same time, as I listened to what was said. It was a humbling moment; one that I will never forget.

Lord, I know You may not often speak to people in a loud voice. You communicate to people in different ways; oftentimes you do so with a *"still, small voice,"*[3] as you did for Elijah, but You spoke loudly to me that day. I thank You for reaching out to me and showing me not only Your power but also Your never-ending compassion.

A Loud Voice

The voice of the Lord is upon the waters,
The God of glory thunders ...
The voice of the Lord is powerful,
The voice of the Lord is majestic.
The voice of the Lord breaks the cedars;
The voice of the Lord hews out flames of fire,
The voice of the Lord shakes the wilderness ...
The voice of the Lord makes the deer to calve
And strips the forests bare;
And in His temple everything says, Glory!
(Psalm 29:3–9 NASB)

April 2013

52

GOD IS FAITHFUL

Just like many other Christians, I can look at my life and say with confidence, "God is faithful." I can now see that even in earlier years when I was questioning my faith, when I was searching and seeking answers, God never deserted me. Before I accepted Christ as my personal Savior at the age of thirty-five, God was there, wooing me and protecting me.

I think back to the time when I was thirty-three and Cyndi, a friend of mine, and I drove up to Idyllwild to meet our other sewing group friends for a girls' getaway weekend. It was dark by the time we headed up the mountain, and as we drew closer to our destination, a fog rolled in. It was difficult for us to see even right in front of the car. We came to a small park and decided to stop to call our friends, hoping they could help us get our bearings (this was before cell phones). There was no one at the park as we headed to a phone booth. However, on our way back to our car, another car suddenly appeared, and two men jumped out, heading directly toward us. We immediately felt threatened. Nervously, I said to Cyndi, "Get back into the car!"

We ran back and quickly got into our seats, closing the doors barely in time. As I reached for the main lock, one of the men came right up to my side of the car. The other man had gone around to Cyndi's side of the car. I remember that just as I engaged the lock, I looked up and made direct eye contact with the man outside my window. In that instant, something happened—something that made him shrink back. He immediately changed course and turned around, calling for his friend to follow him back to their car. I am very aware that anything could have happened that night, as the fog was so thick that no one could have seen. We left the park with our hearts beating fast, feeling so fortunate. We eventually found our way through the fog to meet up with our friends.

As the years have passed and I look back on this frightening experience, I see even more clearly that there was something beyond description that occurred when our perpetrators turned around so abruptly and left. It happened immediately after I made eye contact with the one outside my window. Whether there were angels guarding the door, I don't know. I just feel in my heart that God was present and He was somehow protecting us. Doesn't the Bible say, "*... he will order his angels to protect you wherever you go;*"[1] and that his angels are "*spirit-messengers sent out to help and care for those who are to receive His salvation?*"[2]

Yes, God is faithful. As I continue to try to put Him first and follow after Him, He has made me aware of so much that I wouldn't see if I weren't looking through the eyes of His indwelling Holy Spirit. There have been times when evil has literally jumped right out at me, making me cognizant of its ominous presence and more on guard. God's Holy Spirit keeps me sensitive and alert to what in this world doesn't align with His Word. In fact, the callous, irreverent misuse of His holy name always brings almost physical pain to my grieving heart when it happens.

God has also given me the right words to say at critical times when I could not find them on my own. He continues to give me insights into what I should write about and act upon. Sometimes I am even surprised at how compelled I am to pen my experiences, to create poetry, and to compose songs. God has put the desire in my heart, but I often wonder, if there is a purpose beyond what I can see right now. I do know with assurance that God is good. He has a plan and purpose for not only me but everyone else as well, and He is coming again.

That brings me to write about something that happened a number of years ago that I have never before told anyone or written about but is still very vivid in my mind. It occurred when I was in our driveway, near the rosebushes, getting Katie out of her car seat. She was just a baby at the time, and I was leaning into the car to unbuckle her. I remember detecting a movement on the sidewalk near me, only about eight feet away. I stood up and saw a man who looked like he had walked right out of biblical times. He was wearing a robe of natural woven material, and it was tied with a belt. He had long hair and a full-length beard, and he was carrying a large wooden walking stick as tall as his head. It was such an unexpected and unusual sight; I just stared at him, unable to speak. We just stood and stared at each other for a few seconds, and then he looked right at me, intent on delivering a message: "Repent; the kingdom of God is near." He didn't say anything else.

I still couldn't manage to say anything. I thought I must be dreaming; the whole thing seemed so otherworldly. I didn't want to continue staring, so I leaned into the car again to get Katie. By the time I picked her up and stood up again, which took very little time, this man was standing on the opposite corner, kitty-corner to our house, about 150 feet away, facing me. He then turned as if he were going to walk farther down the street. I glanced away for a second, and when I looked back again, he was gone! I thought to myself, *Where did he go?*

I ran to the corner so I could look all the way down the long street. He was nowhere to be seen! He had completely vanished! I was stunned—dumbfounded! I thought to myself, *There's no way he could move that fast!*

Did this really happen? It all seemed so unreal, and yet why would I ever concoct something like this in my own imagination? I couldn't bring myself to tell anyone. I didn't think anyone would believe me. But the reality is that I know it happened. And now that years have passed, I feel certain that this man (angel?) did come from another dimension to give warning. He came with the same message that I have read since, with awe, a number of times in the Bible (NASB):

- *Isaiah the prophet prophesized,* "The voice of him that cryeth in the wilderness *Prepare ye the way of the Lord Make straight in the desert a highway for our God.*" (Isaiah 40:3)
- *Matthew wrote, "In the days John the Baptist came, preaching in the wilderness of Judea, saying, 'Repent for the kingdom of heaven has come near.'"* (Matthew 3:1–2)

> *"After being baptized by John and overcoming temptation by the devil in the wilderness, Jesus began his ministry by preaching and saying 'Repent for the kingdom of heaven is at hand.'"(4:17)*
>
> *"Jesus sent His disciples out and instructed them: 'And as you go, preach, saying, The kingdom of heaven is at hand.'"(10:7)*
>
> - *Mark stated,* "'The time has come,' (Jesus) said. 'The kingdom of God has come near. *Repent and believe the good news!'"* (Mark 1:15)

Another discovery that startled me when I read the gospel of Matthew was its description of John the Baptist: *"John himself had a garment of camel's hair and a leather belt around his waist ..."* (3:4). I couldn't help thinking about the man (?) I had seen when I read this.

Giving thought to what he said, I did some Bible investigating. There are sixty-eight Bible verses that refer to the kingdom of God in the New Testament. It was a central message preached by John the Baptist, Jesus, and His disciples. The phrase "The kingdom of God is near," or similarly, "The kingdom of God is at hand," has a couple interpretations. The most common understanding is that the realm where God dwells is here and now when we repent of our sins and receive our new life in Christ. It is a reality now! What is *"the world's sin?"* Jesus said it *"is unbelief in Me."*[3] The moment we believe, God makes us *"alive together with Christ"*[4] and *"seat(s) us with Him in the heavenly places."*[5]

However, when this messenger I encountered said, "Repent, the kingdom of God is near," I really felt he was warning me (and everyone) about future events—that Christ will be returning in power and that we all need to make sure we are ready when that happens; that we all will be with Him. There was an urgency in his voice that told me we need to prepare ourselves. It was as if the *"Spirit of truth"* Jesus promised us in the Bible was speaking through this man, to *"guide (us) into all the truth"* and to *"disclose to (us) what is to come."* [6]

The kingdom of God, in and through His Son, Jesus Christ, continues to be the main message God delivered in the past and continues to convey to people everywhere today. The crucial question for everyone is, will you be a part of it? Every person needs to make that critical decision, which will determine his or her destiny; it's a decision that cannot be delayed.

Lord, You are not slow about Your promise to come again, but You are patient, *"not wishing for any to perish, but for all to come to repentance."*[7] You will *"not give up,"* but will plead for us to return to You, and You *"will keep on pleading even with (our) children's children in the years to come."*[8] The question is, how much longer, Lord? "The kingdom of God is near."

I praise and thank you, Lord, for Your faithfulness, Your patience, and Your provision for our eternal future. Your kingdom, Your power, and Your glory are forever and ever! Amen!

May 2013

Though completed, why did *God in My Life* sit untouched for so many months? I now know the answer. Today my thirty-four-year-old son, Kevin, and I sat together on our family room couch, and he opened his heart to receive Christ as his personal Savior. This has always been God's plan for his life and is the answer to many years of fervent prayer on his behalf. This joyous moment, so worthy of much praise and celebration, was also meant to be the last thing written in this book. This is not an ending, but a new beginning.

July 21, 2014

If you believe, you will see the glory of God.

—John 11:40

Bible Translations

Scripture quotations used in this book have been taken from the following Bible versions:

ESV – The Holy Bible: English Standard Version Bible
   Wheaton, IL: Crossway (2001)

KJV – King James Version

MSG – The Message: The Bible in Contemporary Language
   Colorado Springs, CO: Navpress (1993)

NASB – New American Standard Bible
   Anaheim, CA: Foundation Press (1973)

NIV – New International Version
   Colorado Springs, CO: International Bible Society (1973)

NKJV – New King James Version
   Nashville, TN: Thomas Nelson, Inc. (1982)

NLT – New Living Translation
   Wheaton, IL: Tyndale House Publishers (1996)

LB – The Living Bible
   Wheaton, IL: Tyndale House Publishers (1979)

Endnotes

Introduction
1. Deuteronomy 4:9 (LB)
2. Psalms 77:11 (NASB)
3. Psalm 102:18 (LB)

#1
1. Joshua 2:11 T(LB)
2. Isaiah 40:28c (LB)
3. Jeremiah 29:13 (LB)

#4
1. Romans 8:38–39 (LB)

#5
1. Matthew 24:14 (LB)
2. Rick Warren, *Purpose Driven Life* (Grand Rapids, MI: Zondervan, 2002), 655–56 (hereafter cited as *Purpose Driven Life*).

#6
1. Jeremiah 33:25 (LB)
2. Joshua 10:13 (LB)
3. 2 Kings 20:8–11
4. Matthew 27:45 (LB)
5. Matthew 27:51 (LB)
6. Acts 16:26 (NASB)
7. Isaiah 55:9
8. Psalms 16:8 (NASB)

#9
1. John 8:47
2. 1 Corinthians 2:11 (NLT)
3. 1 Corinthians 2:12 (NLT)
4. John 14:26 (NASB)
5. Deuteronomy 5:31 (NASB)
6. Psalm 46:10a (NIV)

#11
1. 1 Corinthians 2:13 (LB)
2. Galatians 5:19–22 (LB)

#14
1. Galatians 2:10 (NASB)
2. Matthew 22:39 (NASB)
3. Titus 3:2 (NASB)
4. Titus 2:14 (NASB)
5. Acts 20:35 (NASB)

#15
1. 2 Corinthians 6:2 (NASB)
2. Revelations 21:5 (NASB)

#17
1. Psalm 147:11
2. Luke 10:27
3. Romans 3:22 (NLT)

#18
1. Psalm 139:2
2. Psalm 139:4

#20
1. Mark 6:51b–52 (LB)
2. Mark 8:17b–18a (LB)
3. John 7:5 (LB)
4. John 9:25c (NASB)
5. Matthew 7:7 (NASB)

#21
1. Romans 3:23 (NASB)
2. Romans 3:10 (NASB)
3. Acts 9:18 (LB)
4. Acts 9:21a (LB)
5. Acts 15:11b (LB)

#22
1. Hebrews 4:12 (NLT)
2. John 6:63b (ESV)

#24
1. Max Lucado, *And the Angels Were Silent* (Sisters, OR: Multnomah Publishers, Inc., 995), 142.
2. Matthew 25:40 (NIV)

#25
1. Romans 10:10a (LB)

#26
1. 1 Timothy 4:7b–8a (LB)
2. Mark 1:35
3. Luke 5:16
4. Acts 17:27
5. 2 Timothy 1:7 (NASB)

#27
1. Matthew 28:18 (LB)
2. 1 Corinthians 12:3
3. *Purpose Driven Life*, 206
4. Ephesians 6:11–12 (LB)
5. Ephesians 6:13 (LB)
6. 2 Corinthians 4:4 (NASB))

#28
1. Matthew 12:30
2. Ephesians 2:2 (LB)
3. 1 John 5:19 (LB)
4. John 12:31 (NASB)
5. 2 Corinthians 4:4 (NASB)
6. Galatians 6:14b (LB)
7. Philippians 3:8b–9a (LB)

#29
1. Galatians 3:28 (NASB)
2. Acts 10:28 (LB)

#30
1. Ephesians 1:17–18 (LB)
2. 1 Thessalonians 5:16–18

#32
1. Luke 10:42 (LB)
2. Luke 12:21 (LB)
3. 1 John 2:17a (NIV)
4. 1 John 2:17b (NIV)
5. John 8:51 (NASB)
6. 2 Corinthians 5:8 (NASB)

#33
1. 1 Peter 2:24a (NASB)

#35
1. James 3:15b–16 (NASB)
2. Proverbs 28:26 (NASB)
3. James 3:17 (NASB)

4. Romans 12:18 (NIV)
5. Galatians 5:22–23a

#36
1. Isaiah 43:4a (NASB)
2. Isaiah 43:4
3. Isaiah 43:1
4. Psalm 73:23a
5. Deuteronomy 31:6
6. Ephesians 3:18
7. Genesis 1:27
8. Francine Rivers, *Leota's Garden* (Wheaton, IL: Tyndale House Publishers, Inc., 2004), 161 (hereafter cited as *Leota's Garden*).
9. Cheri Fuller, *When Mother's Pray* (Sisters, OR: Multnomah Publishers, 1997), 84.
10. Ibid., 79.
11. Ibid., 147.
12. 1 Thessalonians 5:16–18 (ESV)
13. Ruth Bell Graham, *Prodigals and Those Who Love Them* (Ada, MI: Baker Books, 2008), 125.
14. *Leota's Garden,* 161
15. Ephesians 2:10

#37
1. Colossians 3:12–14 (NASB)
2. Philippians 2:14 (NASB)
3. Ephesians 2:4–5,8a (NASB)

#39
1. Job 22:21a (KJV)
2. John 16:33 (NASB)
3. Hebrews 4:12 (NASB)
4. Hebrews 4:1 (NASB)
5. Hebrews 4:3b (LB)

#40
1. Jeremiah 15:17b–18 (LB)
2. Jeremiah 15:19 (LB)
3. Job 1:21b (NASB)
4. Job 1:22 (NASB)
5. Jeremiah 17:6 (LB)
6. Jeremiah 17:8 (LB)
7. Jeremiah 18:14–15a (LB)
8. Habakkuk 2:4b (NASB)

#41
1. 2 Peter 1:16 (LB)
2. 2 Peter 1:16–21 (LB)
3. Ann Graham Lots, *My Hearts Cry* (Nashville, Tennessee: W. Publishing Group, 2002), 11.

#42
1. Mark 9:19b (NASB)
2. Mark 16:11b (NASB)
3. Luke 24:11 (NASB)
4. John 7:5 (NASB)
5. Mark 3:21b (NASB)
6. Matthew 13:13–15A (NASB)
7. Acts 26:24 (NIV)
8. 1 Corinthians 1:18 (LB)
9. Jeremiah 29:13
10. Charles Spurgeon, "God's Already at Work," "Charles Spurgeon's Morning and Evening Read, *Bible Gateway*, September 30, 2007. https://www.biblegateway.com/2007/09/30/.
11. Ibid.
12. John 3:8 (LB)
13. 2 Timothy 2:25 (NASB)
14. 1 Peter 1:8a (LB)

#43
1. 1 John 1:8 (NASB)

2. 1 John 1:10 (NASB)
3. Psalm 103:12 (NASB)
4. Jeremiah 31:34b (KJV)
5. John 14:26 (NASB)
6. Beth Moore, *Beloved Disciple* (Nashville, TN: LifeWay Press, 2002), 151.
7. Ibid., 152.
8. Ibid.
9. 1 Timothy 2:5–6a (NASB)
10. 1 John 1:9 (NASB)
11. John 14:6

#44
1. Philippians 1:6

#45
1. Isaiah 11:6
2. Romans 13:10 (LB)

#46
1. 1 Peter 5:7 (NASB)

#47
1. Luke 10:2b (NASB)
2. John 3:8 (LB)
3. John 1:12 (NIV)

#48
1. Amos 3:3 (LB)
2. Ezekiel 36:26–27
3. 1 Corinthians 6:19 (NASB)
4. Luke 17:21b (LB)
5. Titus 3:5 (NASB)

#49
1. Lydia E. Harris, *Preparing My Heart for Grandparenting* (Chattanooga, TN: AMG Publishers, Inc., 2010), 192

2. Isaiah 65:24 (NASB)
3. 1 John 5:14b–15 (NASB)
4. Psalm 130:3–4 (LB)
5. Psalm 66:18 (NIV)
6. Isaiah 59:1–2 (MSG)
7. *Preparing My Heart for Grandparenting,* 192.

#50
1. Matthew 25:21 (NASB)

#51
1. Daniel 10:6b (NASB)
2. Daniel 10:9 (NASB)
3. 1 Kings 19:12b (KJV)

#52
1. Psalm 91:11 (LB)
2. Hebrews 1:14 (LB)
3. John 16:9
4. Ephesians 2:5 (NASB)
5. Ephesians 2:7 (NASB)
6. John 16:13a (NASB)
7. 2 Peter 3:9 (NASB)
8. Jeremiah 2:9b (LB)

About the Author

Barbara Speicher has always enjoyed writing, whether it is personal reflections, poetry, or songs. She graduated with a degree in English, received her teaching credential, and, eventually, her Master's in Education. To help her elementary students learn in a novel and fun way (and others too), she created and produced four educational CDs with original songs and companion workbooks in various subjects under her company name: Learning by Song.

Barbara lives in Tustin, California, with her husband George and enjoys spending time with her three grown children and her two grandsons, who live nearby.

Made in the USA
San Bernardino, CA
08 July 2015